THE EVANGE

in the
Church of England

Edited by
D.N. Samuel

JAMES CLARKE
Cambridge

ISBN 0 227 67834 6

© The Harrison Trust 1979

Published by
James Clarke & Co., Ltd,
7 All Saints' Passage,
Cambridge, CB2 3LS, England.

David Green (Printers) Ltd, Kettering, Northamptonshire

CONTENTS

PREFACE

As it is several years since the Protestant Reformation Society published a major work, it is a great pleasure to see this book sent out, particularly as it comprises papers read to the Society's conference in the ter-jubilee year of the Society's foundation. The Conference was held at the Old Palace, Lincoln, in September, 1977.

It was not possible to consider every period from the Reformation to today at one conference. Particular attention, therefore, was paid to the Reformation and the present, and to the lesser-known periods of the intervening centuries; thus the more frequented paths of the eighteenth century were not examined in a separate paper.

No attempt has been made by the Editor to change the style of the papers, which were of course prepared for oral delivery.

I am very grateful to Mr. D.A. Scales for his assistance in every aspect of the editorial work of preparing these papers for the press.

The prayer of the Editor and of the Society in making these papers more widely available may best be expressed in words taken from the Society's prayer: 'Pour down of the same Holy Spirit upon us, thy unworthy servants, who desire to be the humble instruments in thy hand of maintaining and communicating the principles of that blessed Reformation. Give us grace, O heavenly Father, to lay aside all earthly views, all political and personal feelings; and to unite in one great object; to shew to them that be in error the light of thy truth, and to bring back thy wandering sheep to the fold of the only true Shepherd of their souls.'

D.N.S.

East Ravendale Rectory,
Grimsby.

I. INTRODUCTION

An athlete, before he leaps forward, first retreats a number of paces. In our conference at Lincoln we felt it necessary to do something similar in spiritual terms. Before we could determine the way forward we considered it would be necessary to go back to the roots of evangelicalism and reformed teaching in the Church of England. We found this a profitable exercise, and hope that others, in sharing our enquiries and conclusions, may find them to be of some help also. The value of this exercise may be summarised in these ways.

First, it gives us a sense of identity as evangelicals in the Church of England. In recent years there has been evidence of a crisis of identity amongst evangelical Churchmen. 'What should an evangelical Anglican believe and teach?' was the title of an essay competition a few years ago. 'What is an evangelical?' was the title of an article that appeared recently. This indicates an element of uncertainty about the distinctive marks of evangelicalism. In going back to the English Reformers and their successors we found certain distinctive themes and doctrines which recur in their thinking, and to which those who claim to be evangelicals today must give due weight and attention. These themes are very ably isolated and expounded in the first paper by Mr. Scales. Who can doubt the importance that the Reformers attached to justification by faith, the authority of Scripture, the need for faithful preaching, and the importance of worthy reception of the sacraments? All these have an immediate relevance to evangelicals today, and we must not shrink from applying them to the life of the church as we find it, just as the Reformers themselves sought a reformation in the church under the Word of God.

But this sense of identity extends beyond what we denominate the evangelical constituency to the Church of England as a whole. What we recognise in the Reformers is the teaching of the Church of England. It may at times in the history of the church since the sixteenth century have suffered many reversals, and even at times have been eclipsed, by the incursion of other teachings alien to it, but it has never wholly disappeared or been destroyed. Just as the clouds which cover the sun, or the moon which temporarily hides it, do not mean, except to naive and primitive people, the extinction of the sun; no more do the temporary set-backs which have attended the doctrines of Grace in the Church of England mean their extinction. The Deism and Arianism of the church in the seventeenth and early eighteenth centuries could not accomplish that, for the same doctrines of Grace returned to shine out in all their glory in the Evangelical Awakening.

If God should grant revival to the Church of England today, we should see once again a quickening of interest in those great truths, despite their present eclipse. The important thing is that there should be those, even though they are few in number, who recognise their abiding importance and relevance, and who from love of the truth commit themselves to upholding and promoting them in the life of the church. The teachings of the Reformers are not merely the teachings of evangelicalism but of the Church of England, and only when this faith, from which she has been alienated for a period, is once more recognised and embraced will there be spiritual power and renewal in the church.

Secondly, it gives us a sense of continuity. No one values isolation in matters of faith for its own sake. It is accepted only in the cause of truth, when it is forced upon one, and there is no other course open. Fellowship with others who believe and hold dear the same doctrines as we do is a source of strength. So also is the sense of oneness with godly men in the past. We should value this no less than the fellowship we enjoy with contemporary believers. To know that we are in agreement with great men whom God used in the past to declare his truth reinforces our own faith and resolution.

The evangelical succession is one of truth of doctrine. Roman Catholics and Anglo-catholics make their appeal to a tactual succession which savours more of legalism than the

Gospel. Our appeal is to the foundation upon which the church is built — the teaching of the apostles and prophets, Christ Jesus himself being the chief corner stone. We are concerned to know that we hold the same doctrines as they held. It is for this reason that we trace our pedigree through Reformers and Divines to the Scriptures themselves. The significance of the Reformers is that it was they who brought to light again the great doctrines of Scripture which had been hidden so long. In the words of Tyndale, they dug again the wells of Abraham which had been stopped up by the spiteful Philistines. We believe, therefore, that our oneness with them is of great importance. To find ourselves in serious disagreement with them should lead us to question the rightness of the path we are following.

We are concerned about those evangelicals who, in recent years, appear to suggest that what the Reformers taught is of little consequence, or only of historical interest. We deplore those who speak of the Reformation as a tragedy. This was the language of Tractarianism in the last century, and we can see the fruits of that kind of thinking in the doctrinal error and confusion of the Church of England today. Only a superficial understanding of the oneness or 'unity' of the church before the Reformation could lead to that kind of statement. It was a oneness in error. It was, as Professor James Atkinson has called it, the biggest 'closed shop' in history, in which he who differed from the prevailing ignorance and superstition was put under interdict and ban. The trend of the times in which we live is once more towards a religious 'closed shop', towards one institutional church in which exclusive spiritual power is to be given to a sacerdotal ministry based upon the concept of so-called apostolic succession. Let there be no mistake, ecumenism moves towards exclusiveness and exclusion despite appearances to the contrary. This understanding of unity or oneness we reject as the dream of men to obtain power over others. The oneness we value is oneness in the truth. The continuity we seek is a continuity in the truth. And our affinity with those who in the past have taught the truth, and suffered and laid down their lives for it, is of greater significance and value to us, than any political union or affiliation based upon a spurious notion of tactual succession, especially when the proposed union is with those who have shown by their words and deeds that they are strangers to the Gospel.

Thirdly, it gives us encouragement. The Psalmist said in the midst of hard times, when God seemed to have forsaken his people, 'I will remember the years of the right hand of the most Highest'[1] — the times of God's power and deliverance in the history of Israel, when he had revealed himself as their Saviour in his mighty acts. Similarly when we remember that, though the times are dark now, they have been darker in the past, and yet the power of God has been revealed and his truth has triumphed, we take heart. When Latimer and Ridley went to the stake, it must have seemed to them as if the cause of the Gospel and the Reformation were at an end in England.

Yet Latimer was confident that God would vindicate his truth. He was, no doubt, punishing England for its disobedience, but the time would come when his mercy and truth would be known again. The light which had been kindled would not be put out. As we consider the history of the church and the cause of truth, fewness of numbers are of no account. What matters is faithfulness. Likewise, the lessons of history, especially those of the nineteenth century, should teach us to eschew policy and carnal wisdom, and rest our cause only upon the arm of God. Alliances with other parties and groups to gain some immediate political advantage in the church arise from weakness not strength, they detract from the integrity of our cause, and lead to defection from its ranks. True evangelicalism must stand committed to the Gospel, whatever the consequences might be, and a glance back at the history of our church convinces us of this, and encourages us in believing that this, too, must be the role of evangelicals today.

What, then, should evangelical Anglicans believe and teach? We hope that this book will help to answer that question. It is our conviction that they have clear, definite, and precise doctrines and principles to uphold, which cohere as a body, and are based upon Scripture. This is the distinctive savour of evangelicalism and of the Reformed religion to be found in the formularies and liturgy of the Church of England. If it should lose that savour then, indeed, it would be true that thenceforth it is good for nothing.

II. THE THEOLOGY OF THE ENGLISH REFORMERS A SURVEY OF SOME IMPORTANT THEMES

D.A. Scales, B.A.
Research Student, Corpus Christi College, Cambridge

In considering the Theology of the English Reformers and making the first study in a survey of the Evangelical Succession in the Church of England, the same subject demands attention, both logically and in importance, before all others — the doctrine of the nature and authority of Scripture. This is in no way to lose sight of the fact that the Christian faith is to 'know thee the only true God and Jesus Christ whom thou hast sent',[1] but is to consider one facet of how the God and Father of our Lord Jesus Christ has chosen to reveal himself. In discussing the order of the Church of England's Articles of Religion (the first five of which deal with the Holy Trinity, the sixth and seventh with Scripture), Dr. W.H. Griffith Thomas wrote:

> In a sense we say first of all, 'I believe in God,' before we bear our testimony to the Scripture as the Word of God. But inasmuch as our faith in God in this sense is only concerned with the conviction of His existence, and of a revelation from Him, the true spiritual order is, 'I believe God has spoken through His Word,' and then, 'I examine that Word to see Who and what God is, and what He has said and done.'[2]

The theology of the Reformers, as epitomised for example in the Thirty-nine Articles, is clearly one which accepts that Scripture is itself the Word of God — that what Scripture says, God says — infallible, inerrant, and supreme in authority in matters of faith. Full discussion of this is not necessary, inasmuch as both those who accept the Reformers' view and those who deny it, appear to agree that this is what the Reformers taught. Hence the Archbishops' Commission on Christian Doctrine, in its report on *Subscription and Assent to the 39 Articles*, stated with regard to the Articles:

the Articles assume that the holy Scriptures are, essentially
and throughout, divine instruction in writing. It is beyond
dispute that when they speak of Scripture as 'God's Word
written' (Article 20) it is this that they mean .... It involved
holding that God teaches by statement and command, and
in this sense that revelation involves conceptual
communication, so that faith requires an irreducible
minimum of correct belief. It involves viewing the
inspiration of the canonical Scriptures as analogous
throughout to that claimed for, and by, the Old Testament
prophets, who were held to be men charged and enabled by
God to speak as from him. It involves maintaining that the
work of the Holy Spirit as interpreter is to enable us to grasp
and integrate the diversified divine teaching of the various
biblical books, and to make it the frame of reference in
terms of which all questions and claims about ultimate
truth and value are themselves questioned and judged. It
involves conceiving reformation of the Church by the Word
of God as requiring an ever-closer conformity of thought,
worship, and conduct to the material content of the biblical
revelation.[3]

The Reformers' doctrine is clear — and is none other than
Scripture's own doctrine of Scripture: the Scriptures are
'God's Word written' (Article 20); they contain all things
necessary to salvation (Article 6); their authority is supreme
so that the Creeds are received because 'they may be proved
by most certain warrants of holy Scripture' (Article 8); the
Church may not ordain anything that is contrary to God's
Word written (Article 20 and 34); and an error is condemned
because it is 'grounded upon no warranty of Scripture, but
rather repugnant to the Word of God' (Article 22). The
Reformers held this teaching in an integrated mind — being
determined to apply it fully.

The Scriptures are God's Word written and are infallible.
Ridley asserted the sovereignty of Scripture in all matters of
faith: 'Mine answer here is taken out of the plain words of St.
Paul, which doth manifestly confound this fantastical
invention .... But what can crafty invention, subtilty in
sophisms, eloquence or fineness of wit, prevail against the
unfallible word of God?'[4] Jewel applied this authority to the
teaching of the church: 'like as the errors of the clock be
revealed by the constant course of the sun, even so the errors

of the church are revealed by the everlasting and infallible word of God.'[5]

It needs then to be stated clearly — or, rather, restated, since this has ever been the teaching of the Reformers and their legitimate successors — that the authentic teaching of the Church of England was and is[6] that the Bible is the true and infallible Word of God, from which the church must derive, and by which the church must reform, all doctrine. Men are called to accept the Bible's own teaching as to its nature and authority, and to seek to apply it to themselves corporately and individually.

The Biblical doctrine of Scripture remains under attack: Professor James Barr's *Fundamentalism* is a full-scale attack on the Reformation position. Professor Barr is outspoken in his conclusion: 'the question for the churches is how far they can recognize fundamentalist attitudes, doctrines and interpretations as coming within the range of what is acceptable to the church.' [7]

Sometimes the doctrine is ignored rather than rebuffed. It was disturbing that the Anglican-Roman Catholic International Commission attempted its work by the perhaps novel, and certainly unsatisfactory, method of erecting the roof of the building first, and then proceeding to the foundations. Thus it was that a statement on the 'Eucharist' appeared first (1971); then on Ministry (1973); and most recently on Authority in the Church (1977). This last is, however, a discussion (and one which leaves much to be desired[8]) of episcopacy in general and the papacy in particular. The meaning of the references to Scripture is elusive:

the inspired documents in which this is related came to be accepted by the Church as a normative record of the authentic foundation of the faith. To these the Church has recourse for the inspiration of its life and mission; to these the Church refers its teaching and practice. Through these written words the authority of the Word of God is conveyed.[9]

The key issue remains undiscussed — the doctrine of Scripture. The reports represent an attempt to synthesize views held by modern Anglican and Roman theologians — not an attempt to find a common mind in submission to the teaching of the Word of God. Cranmer set down the Reformers' methodology:

> that so the contention on both parties may be quieted and ended, the most sure and plain way is to cleave unto holy scripture: wherein whatsoever is found, must be taken for a most sure ground, and an infallible truth; and whatsoever cannot be grounded upon the same, touching our faith, is man's device, changeable and uncertain.[10]

It is frequently asserted that the Church of England's appeal has always been to scripture, tradition, and reason; this is ambiguous (as it usually fails to classify the inter-relationship of the three) and erroneous (as it cannot be asserted from the Church's formularies). This is an attempt to legitimize tradition and reason as authorities and to free them from submission to Scripture; and to authenticate the *status quo* in the Church of England by asserting the three in a loose relationship. Indeed, at the start of the 1970s four writers were prepared to assert: 'Scripture and Tradition are thus from every standpoint not antithetical, but complementary as means of leading us to Christ.'[11] Yet the historic position of our Church is clear, and quite distinct from these assertions. Truth and loyalty to God's Word demand that the Reformation doctrine of Scripture is fearlessly proclaimed today; if only rarely, feebly, or incidentally asserted, it is not being maintained.

It is disappointing that opportunities to assert the evangelical position against modernism, where in particular the Biblical doctrine of Scripture needs proclamation, application, and defence today, have not been used. A critique of the Nottingham National Evangelical Anglican Congress in 1977 stated:

> Of course scholarly and critical insights have their uses, but we must be wary of confusing legitimate and scholarly *methods* with the fundamentally anti-Christian *philosophies* which have used these methods to create 'modern' theology. Christian scholars are not free to pursue any chosen fantasy; like all believers, they are under command to obey Christ in all things.[12]

May a voice that is lacking be supplied, in humbly but fearlessly asserting the Reformed doctrine of Scripture. Scholars need to accept the Bible for what it is — the Word of God — if they are rightly to interpret it. Scholarly and critical insights may have their uses, but it must be stated that these uses are essentially auxiliary, and have proved to be small. The effects of criticism have usually been destructive, both individually and generally; Dr. J.I. Packer wrote in 1958:

> A century of criticism has certainly thrown some light on the human side of the Bible — its style, language, composition, history and culture; but whether it has brought the Church a better understanding of its divine message than Evangelicals of two, three and four hundred years ago possessed is more than doubtful. It is not at all clear that we today comprehend the plan of salvation, the doctrines of sin, election, atonement, justification, new birth and sanctification, the life of faith, the duties of churchmanship and the meaning of Church history, more clearly than did the Reformers, or the Puritans, or the leaders of the eighteenth-century revival.[13]

Whence is the widespread unbelief of today? Whence is the impotence of the Church today? Whence is the stunted and enfeebled evangelicalism — sometimes so misfigured as to be barely recognizable — of today? Confidence in, knowledge of, and obedience to the Scripture has declined. The Reformers' doctrine of Scripture — which is but the Scripture's own doctrine — needs to be recovered not only in theory but in practice. Not until there is a return to full acceptance of the Bible as God's Word in the Reformers' sense, not until there is a fuller, deeper, more painstaking knowledge of that Word, not until the Scripture's doctrines are more adequately preached, applied, obeyed, and acted upon, can there be reasonable hope of a revival of Biblical Christianity.

The Perspicuity of Scripture

But can the Scripture be understood? In answer to this question, the Reformers taught, from Scripture, the doctrine of the perspicuity of Scripture: that the Scripture is clear and lucid in what it states and teaches.

Interpretation of Scripture — hermeneutics — is a matter which is currently absorbing much theological attention. A great emphasis on the difficulty of interpretation appears in much current writing; for instance, the Church of England Doctrine Commission's last report, *Christian Believing,* has a chapter entitled 'The Pastness of the Past', in which questions such as the following are asked:

Can we today genuinely share the thoughts and feelings of
the first readers of St. Paul's Epistles as they were urged to
see in the events of the gospel their own liberation from the
total determination of their lives by astral or planetary
powers?... Can we really be sure that we are understanding
even the words of Jesus in the Gospels in the spirit in which
they were originally intended?[14]

At the Nottingham congress (1977) this subject was
discussed. The writer of the critique previously quoted made
this comment on *The Nottingham Statement*:

we find vagueness and uncertainty at the very heart of our
faith, in the section on *Understanding the Bible Today*. The
influence of the 'new hermeneutic' on sections D2 and D3 is
both obvious and potentially disastrous. Instead of
concentrating on the transcendent wonder of God's timeless
revelation we are told that first we must lock ourselves
within the 'horizon' of the writers of scripture and then leap
from there to the 'horizon' of the modern hearer.[15]

Through this intellectual darkness shines the doctrine of the
perspicuity of Scripture. The *locus classicus* of this doctrine in
the English Reformers is a section in Whitaker's *Disputation
on Scripture*:

the question arises, whether those sacred scriptures, which
we are commanded to search, are so full of obscurity and
difficulty as to be unintelligible to us; or whether there be
not rather a light and clearness and perspicuity in
scripture, so as to make it no useless task for the people to be
engaged and occupied in their perusal. Here, therefore, we
have to dispute concerning the nature of scripture.[16]

The Reformers did not assert that there are *no* difficulties or
obscurities in Scripture, and that all is easy and plain; in view
of the current discussion it is important that this facet of the
Reformers' teaching is held in view. Jewel wrote:

Certain places in the scriptures have evermore been judged
dark, both for many other causes, and also for the matter
itself, and for the deep mysteries therein contained; which
thing D. Luther also hath confessed in sundry places. But
unto them that have eyes and cannot see, and delight more
in darkness than in the light, the sun-beams may seem
dark ....

Certainly, notwithstanding a few certain places in the
holy scriptures be obscure, yet generally 'the scriptures are

a candle to guide out feet;' generally 'God's commandment is light, and lighteth the eyes;' and therefore generally the word of God is full of comfort.[17]

Even though there may be difficulties within the Scriptures, yet no dogma is obscure, but plainly set forth. So a passage in one homily declares: 'Although many things in the Scipture be spoken in obscure mysteries, yet there is nothing spoken under dark mysteries in one place but the selfsame thing in other places is spoken more familiarly and plainly to the capacity both of learned and unlearned.'[18] In dealing with this aspect of the doctrine of perspicuity Whitaker quoted Luther at length:

Luther, in his assertion of the articles condemned by Leo X., in the preface, says that the scripture is its own most plain, easy, and certain interpreter, proving, judging, and illustrating all things. This is said by him most truly, if it be candidly understood. The same author, in his book of the Slavery of the Will against the Diatribe of Erasmus, writes almost in the beginning, that in the scriptures there is nothing abstruse, nothing obscure, but that all things are plain. And because this may seem a paradox, he afterwards explains himself thus: he confesses that many places of scripture are obscure, that there are many words and sentences shrouded in difficulty, but he affirms nevertheless that no dogma is obscure; as for instance, that God is one and three, that Christ hath suffered, and will reign for ever, and so forth. All which is perfectly true: for although there is much obscurity in many words and passages, yet all the articles of faith are plain.[19]

And again:

that God is one in substance and three in persons, that God was made man, and suchlike, although they be in themselves, if we regard the nature of the things themselves, so obscure that they can by no means be perceived by us; yet they are proposed plainly in scripture, if we will be content with that knowledge of them which God hath chosen to impart to us.[20]

Whitaker also argued that to suggest that the Scriptures were other than perspicuous would entail an impious attitude to the work of the Holy Spirit:

If the scriptures be so obscure and difficult to be understood, that they cannot be read with advantage by the people, then this hath happened, either because the Holy Spirit could not write more plainly, or because he would not. No one will say that he could not: and that he would not, is repugnant to the end of writing; because God willed that they should be written and committed to letters for the very end, that we should learn what was written, and thence derive a knowledge of his will.[21]

The nature of the Scriptures is such that learned and unlearned, babes and mature may read them with profit; the perfect Triune God has fashioned a perfect vehicle whereby he may speak to all men. Because of its perspicuity none may fail to see its gospel and main doctrines; but there is material for continual growth in knowledge and understanding. Jewel wrote in his dispute with Harding:

His reason standeth thus: The simple people understandeth not the deep meaning of the psalms; *ergo*, they understand nothing in the psalms. By this key M. Harding may happen to shut out himself .... For albeit the people understand not all the high mysteries of the scriptures, yet it followeth not therefore they understand nothing in the scriptures. For in the scriptures there is both strong meat for men, and also milk for children; 'and in the same,' saith St. Gregory, 'the elephant may swim, and the lamb may wade afoot.'[22]

The illustration of the elephant and the lamb — emphasising Scripture's divine suitability for all needs — is a favourite one with the Reformers.[23] One of the Homilies makes the same point:

And concerning the hardness of Scripture, he that is so weak that he is not able to brook strong meat, yet he may suck the sweet and tender milk, and defer the rest until he wax stronger and come to more knowledge .... And the Scripture is full, as well of low valleys, plain ways, and easy for every man to walk in, as also of high hills and mountains, which few men can climb unto.[24]

Whitaker summed up the Reformers' teaching on perspicuity as follows:

First, that the scriptures are sufficiently clear to admit of their being read by the people and the unlearned with some fruit and utility. Secondly, that all things necessary to salvation are propounded in plain words in the scriptures. Meanwhile, we concede that there are many obscure places, and that the scriptures need explication; and that, on this account, God's ministers are to be listened to when they expound the word of God, and the men best skilled in scripture are to be consulted.[25]

The Lord's Death and the Lord's Supper

One area in which reform according to the teaching of Scripture was greatly required was that of the doctrine of Christ's death, of the Sacrament of the Lord's Supper — which proclaims Christ's death, and of the liturgy used for the administration of the Lord's Supper.

The Reformers taught that Jesus Christ suffered death upon the cross for our redemption, and that — in the familiar words of the Book of Common Prayer — he 'made there (by his one oblation of himself once offered) a full, perfect, and sufficient sacrifice, oblation, and satisfaction, for the sins of the whole world.' The Reformers — particularly Thomas Cranmer, the chief architect of the Book of Common Prayer — designed a liturgy that should express clearly and fully this doctrine of the cross. The care taken was great, the attention to detail minute, the concern to express Biblical doctrine exact.

The order for Holy Communion in the 1549 Prayer Book drew many complaints, though Cranmer intended it to be a purified rite. Gardiner said it was 'Catholic'; Reformers complained of it. So the whole work was revised — it is at least possible that Cranmer had further ideas for revision in mind when the 1549 Book was published — and the order for the Lord's Supper in the 1552 Prayer Book became, with only a few small changes, the service of the Church of England's Prayer Book today. The number, nature, and detail of the changes made in 1552 reveal the care, thought, and anxiety which Cranmer had for faithfulness to Scripture. All ambiguity, all that had been mis-taken, was removed: to take one of the many possible examples, all references to any sacrifice but the once-for-all sacrifice of Christ were removed from the text before the partaking of communion, and placed after this, where they were an appropriate and unambiguous reference to the only sacrifice which a Christian can offer — one of praise and thanksgiving in response to the Father's free grace in the saving death of Christ. Gregory Dix's assessment of the 1552 order, though perhaps the most hackneyed quotation of liturgiology, deserves repetition:

Compared with the clumsy and formless rites which were evolved abroad, that of 1552 is the masterpiece of an artist. Cranmer gave it a noble form as a superb piece of literature, which no one could say of its companions; but he did more. As a piece of liturgical craftsmanship it is in the first rank — once its intention is understood. It is *not* a disordered attempt at a catholic rite, but the only effective attempt ever made to give liturgical expression to the doctrine of 'justification by faith alone'.[26]

The immense influence of this order is in danger of being overlooked. This is not a reference to the beauty of its language, nor to the affection which may be felt for it by those who have used it in England and throughout the world. Its potency as a force for teaching Biblical doctrine is where its greatest influence and achievement lies. As often as men and women have attended this service, the Bible's teaching on the cross and its saving power has been spelt out to them, and a fitting context provided for them to obey the Lord's command to 'Take, eat', remembering his death for them. In times and places where the ministry has not been faithful to Scripture, where the preaching has not agreed with the doctrines of our Church, where the doctrine of substitutionary atonement has been cast aside and mocked, the liturgy has yet brought home to its users the scriptural teaching on the Cross. It need hardly be said what an enfeebling and corrupting effect a liturgy which taught error, or was vacuous and unmeaningful, would have had on its users. The same is true today.

The Reformers put doctrine first; of its essential primacy they were convinced. After they were content that the doctrine was pure, they might ask questions about order, expediency of design and wording, and other matters; but doctrine came first. Such a striving after true doctrine should mark the attempts at liturgical revision today. Dr. Packer wrote powerfully on this issue in 1966:

It is necessary, therefore, to insist that any proposed new forms of worship must submit to a doctrinal test, and to be clear in our minds that no compensating excellences that they may prove to have can make up for doctrinal deficiency, or justify us in using them until such deficiency is remedied. Nor is it enough to ask whether proposed new forms actually contradict the gospel.... What we should ask is whether ... the new forms represent the clearest and most potent liturgical expression of the gospel, appropriately applied, that we can envisage for each occasion. Only when our minds are satisfied on this point can we justify ourselves in experimenting with them to see if they are effective in use.[27]

It behoves those who are the Reformers' successors in this generation — whose evangelical succession is not one by any form of tangible connection, but one of agreement in the Biblical Gospel recovered at the Reformation — to follow out the Reformers' principles. By these all the 'experimental' communion liturgies (Series 1, Series 2, and Series 3) stand condemned; their doctrine is deficient, whether by simple error or omission of the truth.

The Reformers saw the sacrament of the Lord's Supper as God speaking to man — the essential movement was from God to man, and was epitomised in the Homily's caution that 'We must then take heed, lest, of the memory, it be made a sacrifice'.[28] The sacrament was a visible word from God to man, confirming the Word preached. The remembrance (*anamnesis*) came from eating and drinking the bread and wine; the Lord's command to 'Do this in remembrance of me' was fulfilled by eating and drinking, and not by offering the elements to God, or praying over them. God's grace was displayed.

Yet how does the Series 3 Communion service compare with the Biblical teaching on the Lord's Supper, which the Reformers were at such pains to set forth clearly? Certain aspects only can be considered.

Any statement of the substitutionary atonement of the Lord Jesus Christ on the Cross is absent, not only explicitly, but implicitly in the whole ethos of the service. 'We celebrate and proclaim his perfect sacrifice made once for all upon the cross' is not of itself a statement of substitutionary atonement. This absence is most serious. Not only so, but the service is said to be a celebration and proclamation of other mighty acts of God: whereas the Scripture is clear that when we eat the bread and drink the wine we proclaim the Lord's death. Our Lord Jesus Christ instituted a 'perpetual memory of that his precious death'. It is a serious disobedience to Biblical teaching, and makes a nonsense of the sacrament (for the bread and wine can hardly in any easy sense be said to represent, for example, the ascension), to turn it aside from Christ's death.

Godward references now occur in the prayer of consecration, misdirecting the sacrament: 'Accept our praises, heavenly Father, through your Son, our Saviour Jesus Christ; ... Accept through him, our great high priest, this our sacrifice of thanks and praise'. The portrayal of God's free grace is vitiated, as man in his pride must needs contribute to his salvation. The severe strictures which Dr. Packer applied to Series 1 and Series 2 in draft apply to the final text of all three experimental forms:

But it is a different matter when both prayers offer to God the Church's sacrifice of praise ... as a preliminary to communion. This makes God's sacramental gift to us proceed on the basis of our gift to Him, and the fundamental movement of the Eucharist becomes man's movement Godward instead of God's movement manward. This return from the pattern of Cranmer's 1552 rite to that of its 1549 predecessor expresses a mistaken doctrine either of atonement and justification, as events to which the Church contributes, or of the sacrament, as a significant sign of Christian worship rather than of the Christian gospel.... this treatment of the Supper, however it be interpreted theologically, effectively obscures its biblical character as 'a Sacrament of our Redemption by Christ's death', and of the grace of the new covenant whereby helpless sinners receive full and free forgiveness through Christ alone, by faith alone, without our own work or merit contributing anything. This is so basic a distortion of the biblical meaning of the Supper as to make both rites unacceptable.[29]

To those who love the Scripture's doctrine of the Lord's Supper, to those who share the Reformers' earnest desire that full and free forgiveness through the atoning sacrificial death of Christ should be proclaimed, to those who wish to be the twentieth-century custodians of the evangelical heritage, the Series 3 order must be unacceptable. In this brief comparison of the Series 3 order with the doctrine and liturgy of the English Reformers certain strands only have been taken as indicators. Many other matters might have been considered, including reservation, prayer for the dead, the *epiclesis*, and deliberate ambiguity. Sufficient has been mentioned to show the unacceptable nature of the Series 3 order.

Worthy Reception

There is one particular aspect of the Reformers' teaching on the doctrine of the Lord's Supper which it is important to draw out, as it is a key point in their theological system and is as much opposed today as it has always been. That is the matter of worthy reception. 'To such as rightly, worthily, and with faith, receive the same, the Bread which we break is a partaking of the Body of Christ; and likewise the Cup of Blessing is a partaking of the Blood of Christ.'[30] Reception of the benefits testified to by the sacrament is conditional: 'to such as rightly, worthily, and with faith, receive the same'. This worthiness is not, of course, any righteousness that the partaker brings with him, but merely the disposition of heart which God requires of him. Bradford dealt with this matter:

> The apostle willeth all men to prove and 'examine themselves before they eat of the bread and drink of the cup; for they that eat and drink unworthily eat and drink damnation;' therefore this probation and examination is necessary.... The true probation and trial of a christian conscience consisteth altogether in faith and repentance. Faith hath respect to the doctrine and articles of our belief: repentance hath respect to manners and conversation.[31]

Without faith there is no participation in the benefits of the Supper, no remembrance of the atoning death of Christ which recalls its benefits to our hearts and minds:

> The Body of Christ is given, taken, and eaten, in the Supper, only after an heavenly and spiritual manner. And the mean whereby the Body of Christ is received and eaten in the Supper is Faith. The Wicked, and such as be void of a lively faith, ... in no wise are they partakers of Christ...[32]

This matter was so central to the Reformers' understanding of the nature, purpose, and use of the Supper, that the petition in the prayer of consecration (which, though it is a long prayer, has only one petition in it) is for right reception:

> Hear us, O merciful Father, we most humbly beseech thee; and grant that we receiving these thy creatures of bread and wine, according to thy Son our Saviour Jesus Christ's holy institution, in remembrance of his death and passion, may be partakers of his most blessed Body and Blood.

This prayer is for the *recipient* — a prayer that as he receives the bread and wine he may also participate in the benefits of the sacrificial death of Christ; because there is no necessary benefit from attendance, and because right, worthy, and faithful reception is required, the prayer is that the recipient may receive the spiritual benefit.

To emphasise this, the Series 3 prayer of consecration may by contrast be examined: the petition in the parallel section of the consecration prayer is 'grant that by the power of your Spirit these gifts of bread and wine may be to us his body and his blood'. The prayer in unreformed liturgies, as in Series 3 (which the pedantic may prefer to call dereformed!), is for the elements, a complete change of emphasis: a change in the elements is prayed for, a sacrament is in view which is efficacious because of its inherent virtue and not because of the state of the recipient, and the worthiness of the recipient is passed over. Yet if such things are pointed out to many evangelicals today, they put their telescopes, Nelson-like, to their closed eye and blandly proclaim, 'I see no false doctrine'.

Jewel treated of this matter:

The merits of Christ's death, whereof we entreat, are conveyed unto us by God, and received by us. God conveyeth them to us only of his mercy; and we receive them only by faith.... The sacraments serve specially to direct and to aid our faith. For they are, as St. Augustine calleth them, *verba visibilia*, 'visible words', and seals and testimonies of the gospel. All this notwithstanding, we say, it is neither the work of the priest, nor the nature of the sacrament as of itself, that maketh us partakers of Christ's death, but only the faith of the receiver. St. Augustine saith: ...'From whence hath the water this great power, that it toucheth the body and washeth the heart, save by the working of the word? Not for that it is pronounced, but for that it is believed.'[33]

As worthy partaking leads to participation in the benefits of the death of Christ, so unworthy partaking brings judgement. The Reformers taught that no benefit resulted to one who came unworthily to the Lord's table; Cranmer, speaking in the disputation of the Sacrament in the House of Lords in December 1548, stated:

They be twoo things to eate the Sacrament and to eate the

bodie of Christ.

The eating of the bodie is to dwell in Christ, and this may be thoo a man never taste the Sacrament.

All men eate not the body in the Sacrament....

I beleave that Christ is eaten with harte.

The eating with our mouth cannot gyve us lief.

Ffor then shulde a synner have lief....

Onely goode men can eate Christ's body. When the evill eateth the Sacrament, Breade and wyne, he neither hath Christ's body nor eateth it.[34]

Jewel illustrated this position:

When one that is unlearned, and cannot read, looketh upon a book, be the book never so true, never so well written, yet, because he knoweth not the letters, and cannot read, he looketh upon it in vain. He may turn over all the leaves, and look upon all, and see nothing; but another that can read, and hath judgment to understand, considereth the whole story, the doughty deeds, grave counsels, discreet answers, examples, promises, threatenings, the very drift and meaning of him that wrote it. So do the faithful receive the fruit and comfort by the sacraments, which the wicked and ungodly neither consider nor receive.[35]

The responsibility which rests on all who come to the Lord's table is that of self-examination. Ridley wrote: 'Oh! how necessary then is it, if we love life and would eschew death, to try and examine ourselves before we eat of this bread and drink of this cup!'[36]

The principle of worthy reception will be an important factor in considering the right place for communion services on Sundays. There has been an increasing movement in many, though by no means all, churches towards 'the practice of a weekly celebration of the sacrament as the central corporate service of the church'.[37]

Much discussion of the place and the use of the sacrament of the Lord's Supper is conducted in weighted language, which assumes that frequent usage and 'centrality' shows greater esteem for this sacrament; reference to the Lord's Supper as the main service of the people of God is debatable, if 'main' is intended to signify that which should be attended each Sunday rather than any other. A right and, indeed, a high esteem of this sacrament is revealed in the theology of the English Reformers, and also in the evangelical

succession; but a true regard is one that agrees with the
teaching of Scripture and makes use of the sacrament as
Scripture requires. Frith wrote: 'For the right honour of a
thing is, to use it for the intent that it was institute of God;
and he that abuseth it to any other purpose, doth indeed
dishonour it.'[38] It seems very doubtful that any teaching
about frequency of reception can be derived from Scripture;
equally the general inference from the Reformers (from the
rubrics of the Prayer Book order) is that it was not thought
likely that people in parish churches would communicate
frequently.

By all means let there be a communion service at some time
each Sunday for those who wish to participate, and also
communion services at main times on occasions so that the
whole church may share together the bread and the wine. But
if in the present situation the Lord's Supper is made *the* main
Sunday service each week, there is great danger of
encouraging many to come to the Lord's Table who would not
of themselves have chosen to and thus encouraging
thoughtless and unworthy participation, of encouraging even
subconsciously ideas of automatic benefit from participation
(*ex opere operato*), and — in practice — of detracting from the
ministry of the Word.

Should Children Come to the Lord's Table?

The suggestion, which has recently been widely broadcast,
that children might be admitted to communion at a younger
age, and then later be confirmed, requires careful
consideration. In 1972 the Rev. C.O. Buchanan wrote:

> Once baptized, children ought to be brought up as
> Christians, and this includes admitting them to Holy
> Communion.... It is easy to sympathize with the Reformers
> who looked back to the superstition in which they had been
> brought up and required understanding of intellectual
> propositions before admission to communion. But there is
> no necessary reason to follow them....[39]

It is ironic that a child may be considered a fit person to come
to the Lord's Table, but not yet fit and mature enough to take
upon himself at confirmation the solemn covenant pledges of
baptism. Our Reformers intended that generally confirmation
should precede admittance to the Lord's Table, as the rubric
at the end of the Confirmation service makes clear: 'And

there shall none be admitted to the Holy Communion, until such time as he be confirmed, or be ready and desirous to be confirmed.' Exceptions are possible, and there is certainly no suggestion that confirmation is of itself an essential prerequisite to admittance; but readiness for confirmation *is* considered by the Reformers as a requirement for admittance to the Lord's Supper. The current suggestion must, therefore, be considered quite foreign to the teaching of the Reformers, and indeed, when considered in their terms, nonsense.

Jewel dealt with the question of infants and young children receiving communion:

> notwithstanding it appear by St Augustine, St Cyprian, and others, that infants in the primitive church in sundry places were admitted to holy communion, yet afterward, upon good advice, they were justly removed from it; because that, being in that age, they were not thought able to examine and prove themselves according to the doctrine of St Paul, and so to eat of that bread, and to drink of that cup. In like sort in the law of Moses, notwithstanding all men-children were commanded to be circumcised, yet none were admitted to eat the passover but only such as could demand what it meant.[40]

Henry Bullinger, the Zurich Reformer whose *Decades* were compulsory reading for many Elizabethan clergy, treated of this question:

> And although that infants are reputed to be of the church and in the number of the faithful, yet are they not capable of the supper.... This was instituted for them that are of lawful years, and not for infants. 'Let a man examine himself,' saith the apostle, 'and let him so eat of the bread, and drink of the cup.' And the Lord saith: 'Do this in the remembrance of me.' And again: 'Shew forth the Lord's death until he come.' All which sayings take place in people of lawful years, not in infants.[41]

In another place, when discussing Paul's command, Bullinger wrote: 'Whereby all men understand that the eucharist, or sacrament of the Lord's supper, is for them to receive that are of perfect age, and not for infants.'[42]

Among the visitation articles prepared for the provincial visitation of Edmund Grindal in 1576 is the following:

> Whether your parson, vicar, curate, or minister hath admitted to the holy Communion any of his parish, being

above twenty years of age, either mankind or womankind, that cannot say by heart the Ten Commandments, the Articles of the Faith, and the Lord's Prayer in English, and what be the names of such as cannot say the same, or being above fourteen years and under twenty years of age, that cannot say the Catechism allowed and set forth in the said book of Common Prayer.[43]

The inference from this article is that Grindal did not expect anybody in the province of Canterbury to be admitted to the Holy Communion who was not at least fourteen years old.

The judgement of the Reformers was that infants and children should not be admitted to the Lord's Supper. In an excellent article, which gives careful consideration to a wide range of evidence, the Rev. R. T. Beckwith has argued persuasively against child communion:

It therefore seems that the deferment of admission to communion (as well as confirmation) until the candidate becomes an adult is the course which accords best with Christ's institution, and this being so, there is no reason to fear that children or infants will suffer any loss by not being admitted to communion earlier.[44]

Two factors have conspired to bring circumstantial pressure to bear. It is clear that among some modern evangelical writers on the sacraments and sacramental theology there is a distinct movement towards the *ex opere operato* attitude to the sacraments; this is not to say that the movement is full or in every way explicit, but there can be no doubt about the direction. The authors of *Growing into Union*, who included Dr. Packer and Mr. Buchanan, were prepared to make statements like this about the sacraments:

The language of Scripture about them is the language of sheer unqualified efficacy. If the outward celebration is performed, then on the first showing the inward grace is mediated. Those who have been baptized into Christ 'have put on Christ' (Gal. 3.27). Those who receive communion receive the body and blood of Christ (as the words of institution testify). The simple expectation is that those who partake of the sacraments are partakers in them and by them of God's grace. If there is an occasional warning, such as in 1 Cor. 10, yet the overall picture is one of serene objectivity and confidence on the writers' part in the efficacy of the sacraments.[45]

Even though the authors state soon after that 'Without faith
it is true that a sacrament is not in itself salvific', the change
in emphasis is clear.   So Mr. Buchanan made similar
statements in an essay, 'The Church and Baptism', in 1972:

> The language of the New Testament is undoubtedly that of
> unqualified efficacy — those who have been baptized into
> Christ 'have put on Christ'. Baptism effects what it
> signifies....
>
> There are exceptions to this categorical or unconditional
> language. The most obvious one is in 1 Corinthians 10....
> But such language is exceptional.[46]

Such statements 'so expound one place of Scripture, that it be
repugnant to another'. The New Testament does not teach
that sacraments effect what they signify; its warnings should
not be laid aside as 'occasional' or 'exceptional'. The
teaching of 1 Corinthians 11, and the theme that a man may
be circumcised in the flesh but uncircumcised in heart, make
it clear that the language of Scripture about sacraments is *not*
'the language of sheer unqualified efficacy'.

A second factor is the making in some churches of the
Lord's Supper on Sundays into *the* central (and often family)
service;   this   produces   the   anomalous   position   of
non-communicating attendance by children. The correct
solution to this is to provide some form of ministry
appropriate to children (which the Lord's Supper is not) at the
same time, or, more radically, not to have communion
services in this position on Sundays.

Preaching

The first mark of the visible church of Christ is that it is a
congregation of faithful men 'in the which the pure Word of
God is preached'.[47] Such was the teaching of the English
Reformers. The neglect of preaching had been a characteristic
of the pre-Reformation era, and such as there was was not the
preaching of the *pure* Word of God. The Reformers argued
cogently that preaching was a mark of the true church and
should have a position of primacy in it; the honouring and
frequenting of preaching was a mark of times of blessing, and
the neglect and despising of preaching marked spiritual
dearth. Becon wrote that it 'is the first and principal point of
a bishop's and spiritual minister's office to teach and preach
the word of God'.[48] Latimer never tired of asserting that

preaching was the ordinary means appointed by God to bring men to salvation:

> But some will say now, 'What need we preachers then? God can save his elect without preachers.' A goodly reason! God can save my life without meat and drink; need I none therefore? No, no; I must keep the way that God hath ordained, and use the ordinary means that God hath assigned, and not seek new ways. This office of preaching is the only ordinary way that God hath appointed to save us all by. Let us maintain this, for I know none other; neither think I God will appoint or devise any other.[49]

How this cuts through the shallow thinking of today! Tyndale pointed out that preaching was the God-ordained means of blessing: 'They preach also, that the wagging of the bishop's hand over us blesseth us, and putteth away our sins. Are these works not against Christ? How can they do more shame unto Christ's blood?... The apostles knew no ways to put away sin, or to bless us, but by preaching Christ.'[50] Consequently, as Latimer stressed, the office of preaching must be maintained and furthered:

> Beware, beware, ye diminish not this office; for if ye do, ye decay God's power to all that do believe.
>
> ... we must be ready to hear God's holy word; we must have good affections to hear God's word; and we must be ready to make provision for the furtherance of the preaching of God's holy word, as far forth as we be able to do.[51]

'It belongeth unto a pastor, not so much to have learned many things, as to have taught much', wrote Jewel.[52] Latimer used Christ's example to teach the importance of preaching and the diligence required of preachers: ' "I must preach the kingdom of God to other cities also: I must shew them my Father's will, for I came for that purpose: I was sent to preach the word of God." Our Saviour Christ said, how he must not tarry in one place: for he was sent to the world, to preach everywhere.'[53] Latimer listed the properties of every good preacher: 'to be a true man; to teach, not dreams nor inventions of men, but *viam Dei in veritate*, "the way of God truly;" and not to regard the personage of man.'[54] This last point Latimer developed elsewhere:

> though a preacher be well learned, but yet lacketh that boldness, and is fainthearted, truly he shall do but little

good for all his learning. When he feareth men more than God, he is nothing to be regarded. Therefore this is the thing that St Paul so much desireth, to have boldness to speak: for when a preacher's mouth is stopped, so that he dare not rebuke sin and wickedness, no doubt he is not meet for his office.[55]

Such faithfulness and fearlessness does not issue in popularity, as Sandys noted:

Hard it is to find one fourth, that will love and reverence us as fathers, obey us as governors, honour us as God's embassadors, learn of us as schoolmasters, hear and follow us as shepherds, give us worthy wages as workmen that take pains for your salvation. But our expectation is not deceived: Christ our Saviour hath told us long ago that the world should hate us; and our case is no worse herein than the blessed apostles' was: our reward is great in heaven.[56]

Latimer pointed out in his most famous sermon that the devil is always at work to oppose the true preaching of the Word of God: 'He is the most diligent preacher of all other'.[57] Elsewhere he took up the same theme: 'Here you may see how necessary this office is to our salvation. This is the thing that the devil wrestleth most against: it hath been all his study to decay this office. He worketh against it as much as he can: he hath prevailed too much, too much in it.'[58]

Preaching brings obligations to men to seek to hear. Thus Latimer marked the earnestness with which men sought to hear Christ:

So the people sought out Christ, they smelt his savour; he was a sweet smell to them. He is *odor vitae ad vitam*, 'the smell of life to life.' They flocked about him like eagles.... His doctrine eased the burden of the soul; it was sweet to the common people, and sour to the scribes. It was such comfort and pleasure to them, that they came flocking about him. Wherefore came they? *Ut audirent verbum Dei*. It was a good coming; they came to hear the word of God.[59]

Sandys spoke against dislike of a minister keeping men from hearing the Word: 'If we mislike the minister, shall we mislike the message also? If we cannot brook the messenger, shall we be at defiance with him that sent him?'[60] Latimer had a high view of preaching, and so spoke of the dreadful consequences of despising it:

So likewise in our time, God hath sent light into the world;

he hath opened the gates of heaven unto us by his word; which word be opened unto us by his officers, by his preachers: shall we now despise the preachers? Shall we refuse to hear God's word, to learn the way to heaven, and require him to save us without his word? No, no; for when we do so, we tempt God, and shall be damned world without end.[61]

Is the Reformers' doctrine of preaching maintained today? And, more pointedly, is it maintained and practised by those who claim to be the inheritors of the evangelical succession? Has preaching not suffered an eclipse in our generation? A world in which the influence of dialogue and discussion groups is felt, in which men have so often had their confidence in God's word undermined — sometimes clearly sometimes subtly, in which activism and participation have become a mania, in which a vogue for counselling has appeared, in which shallow thinking and brevity are esteemed — such a world finds that preaching does not fit its temper. Our generation cannot afford to lose the Reformers' clear understanding from Scripture that God has ordained preaching as the ordinary means of salvation and public edification. 'Thus saith the Lord' must be heard, not as a liturgical cliche, but as the mark of pulpit ministry; fashions may change, but God's ordained means have not.

Uncertainty about the ordained ministry marks our church today. One reason for this must be the weakened esteem in which preaching is held. The vision of what preaching can be in the will of God, of the awful solemnity and the excellence of this work, has largely been lost. For the twelve it was their chief task: 'It is not reason that we should leave the word of God'; 'we will give ourselves continually to prayer, and to the ministry of the word.'[62]

The voice of the greatest preacher of the English Reformation sounds in the ears of the Church of England today, and speaks to his evangelical successors:

Beware, beware, ye diminish not this office; for if ye do, ye decay God's power to all that do believe.

I must keep the way that God hath ordained, and use the ordinary means that God hath assigned, and not seek new ways. This office of preaching is the only ordinary way that God hath appointed to save us all by. Let us maintain this, for I know none other; neither think I God will appoint or devise any other.[63]

Conclusion

Any examination of the Theology of the English Reformers brings home the immense importance of true doctrine to them. If God had spoken in the Scripture, then his revealed will was to be sought, known, and obeyed. This basic attitude of Reformation theology is not naturally appreciated today, when synthesis and dedoctrinisation are popular concerns. The definition of such words as 'evangelical' becomes increasingly difficult, indeed virtually impossible, if all who claim the title are to be included. Moreover, there appears to be an unwillingness to define 'evangelical' in terms of doctrine. All this tells, not of the prosperity and vigour, but of the malaise and somewhat effete character, of much contemporary so-called 'evangelicalism'. God has spoken in his Word: a right esteem for Biblical doctrine marked the theology and the attitudes of the English Reformers, and will mark the theology and attitudes of their true successors. A recovery of this love of scriptural doctrine will be a necessary concomitant of any renascence of vital Christianity.

A survey of some aspects of Reformation liturgy points up the Reformers' seriousness of attitude and worship. Dr. P.E. Hughes described it as follows:

> The worship of Almighty God, Creator, Redeemer, and Judge, was for the Reformers not merely an indescribable privilege but also a most solemn responsibility. They approached God with love and joy indeed, but with awe too, for they were ever conscious of His infinite majesty and holiness. To come before God without seriousness was great wickedness.[64]

Yet one of the dangers which is clear today is that of confusing worship with entertainment — the heavenly worship of the thrice-holy God which Isaiah witnessed is replaced by the novel, the sensuous, and the amusing. How this generation needs to hear its Reformation forefathers: 'By their example and by their writings, and particularly by the Book of Common Prayer, the Reformers recall us to worship that is scriptural, that is evangelical, and that is serious.'[65]

A study of Reformation views of preaching reveals an immutable message, the Gospel of our Lord Jesus Christ, which is to be preached, although it may not always be well received by its hearers. Against this must be measured today's fashions for 'involvement', synthesis, and compromise — spurious unity without regard for truth. Latimer declared:

in matters of religion we must take heed that we have such a peace which may stand with God and his word; for it is better to have no peace at all, than to have it with the loss of God's word.

We ought never to regard unity so much that we would, or should, forsake God's word for her sake.[66]

Much of modern ecumenism is weighed and found wanting by this principle; so indeed is the policy advocated by some evangelicals of such 'involvement' with other groups in the Church of England as entails an acceptance of their teaching as legitimate in our Church and a blind commitment to work with them. The heirs of the evangelical succession are called to loyalty to their title-deeds — the Theology of the English Reformers — and to witness faithfully to the distinctiveness of this message from all others which may be set forth in the Church of England today. So, we are fully committed to the Church of England — as she is by her formularies delineated and as she ought to be, not to the *de facto* deviations of the day; but we find true unity and fellowship more with those who share with us the great doctrines of the Scriptures and the Reformation, whatever their denomination, than with members of our own church who reject these doctrines. 'For peace ought not to be redeemed *jactura veritatis*, with loss of the truth; that we would seek peace so much, that we should lose the truth of God's word.'[67]

In finishing, it seems appropriate and timely to recall that most famous dictum of the English Reformation, Latimer's words to Ridley at the stake: 'Be of good comfort, master Ridley, and play the man. We shall this day light such a candle, by God's grace, in England, as I trust shall never be put out.'[68] These words are not only the noble and moving sentiments of a brave man; they also give us a profound insight into the theology of the English Reformers and its outworking. Their willingness to suffer martyrdom emphasises the extent of their conviction of the inspiration and infallibility of Scripture, the nature of the Atonement, the significance of the Sacraments, and the need to bear faithful witness to the message which they preached. They leave an example to their successors: to be willing to witness to the truth at whatever cost. Let those who have an earnest conviction of the truth of the Biblical Gospel stand fast and bear witness, not being distracted by half-truths and compromise.

Latimer and Ridley, and their fellow Reformers, were men of faith — men who believed God and his promises, whatever the nature of outward circumstances. In all the outward difficulties, imminent death, the small number of those standing with him, and the public casting away of the Gospel, Latimer did not lose sight of the fact that the message was God's: he would maintain his work; he would bring it to fruition. So Latimer looked in confidence to the future, that the Gospel would yet flourish in England.

More broadly, the Reformers saw that the work was God's — 'by God's grace'. God is at work, revealing himself, defending his own cause. The fact that all is of the grace of God was their confidence and strength; so may it be for their heirs and successors. The grace of God is sufficient for our day — he can yet revive his work. May he grant that the candle lit by the English Reformers shall, by his grace, burn brightly in this generation, and that it shall never be put out — 'To the praise of the glory of his grace'.[69]

III. TOPLADY'S VIEW OF DOCTRINAL CONTINUITY AFTER THE REFORMATION

The Rev. B.G. Felce, M.A.
Vicar of All Saints', Preston

About the middle of the eighteenth century the celebrated lawyer, Sir William Blackstone, who went to hear every clergyman of note in London, stated that

> he did not hear a single discourse which had more Christianity in it than the writings of Cicero, and that it would have been impossible for him to discover, from what he heard, whether the preacher were a follower of Confucius, of Mahomet, or of Christ![1]

Perhaps there is some exaggeration here, but there is no doubt of the moral degradation of the times.

In 1736 Bishop Butler wrote in the Advertisement to his *Analogy of Religion*:

> It is come, I know not how, to be taken for granted, by many persons, that Christianity is not so much as a subject of inquiry; but that it is, now at length, discovered to be fictitious. And accordingly they treat it, as if, in the present age, this were an agreed point among all people of discernment; and nothing remained, but to set it up as a principal subject of mirth and ridicule, as it were by way of reprisals, for its having so long interrupted the pleasures of the world.[2]

It was in this spiritual climate that a small number of evangelicals preached the doctrines of the Bible and of the Reformed Church of England and had an influence out of all proportion to their number. The latter end of the century saw a large increase in the number of evangelical clergy and a great change for the better in the spiritual and moral condition of the country. The great majority of evangelicals held Calvinistic opinions like those of George Whitefield. Their views were largely those of the Reformers of the sixteenth century and of the Puritans of the seventeenth century. They loved the Thirty-nine Articles and the Homilies. But unlike the Puritan the evangelical was satisfied with the Book of Common Prayer and with government by bishops and wished to remain within the National Church. Thus William Grimshaw (1708-63), Vicar of Haworth, wrote to Charles Wesley that he believed 'the Church of England to be the soundest, purest, and most apostolical well-constituted national Christian Church in the world.'[3]

Augustus Toplady was ordained in 1762 and died in 1778 at the early age of thirty-eight. He was Vicar of Broad Hembury in Devon from 1768 until his death. His most important book, entitled *Historic Proof of the Doctrinal Calvinism of the Church of England*, was published in 1774. Bishop Ryle spoke highly of this book and declared that it is unanswerable. This

is a treatise that displays a prodigious amount of research and reading. It is a book that no one could have written who had not studied much, thought much, and thoroughly investigated an enormous mass of theological literature. You see at once that the author has completely digested what he has read, and is able to concentrate all his reading on every point which he handles. The best proof of the book's ability is the simple fact that down to the present day it has never been really answered. It has been reviled, sneered at, abused, and held up to scorn. But abuse is not argument. The book remains to this hour unanswered, and that for the simplest of all reasons, that it is unanswerable. It proves irrefragably, whether men like it or not, that Calvinism is the doctrine of the Church of England, and that all her leading divines, until Laud's time, were Calvinists. All this is done logically, clearly, and powerfully. No one, I venture to think, could read the book through, and not feel obliged to admit that the author was an able man.[4]

Today we reject the violent spirit and language which Toplady sometimes used when speaking of his opponents, but this does not detract from the worth of his arguments.

Toplady's principles are revealed in what his biographer says about his subscription to the Articles, Homilies, and Liturgy. Toplady mentioned that 'he did not believe them because he subscribed them, but subscribed them because he believed them.'[5] Well would it be for the Church of England if there were more clergy today who believed in the Biblical doctrines of the Articles, Homilies, and Liturgy.

Toplady lived in very close communion with God. Bishop
Ryle wrote of him: 'I hardly find any man of the last century
who seems to have soared so high and aimed so loftily, in his
personal dealings with his Saviour, as Toplady. There is an
unction and savour about some of his remains which few of
his contemporaries equalled, and none surpassed.'[6]

In the Advertisement to his great work Toplady defines the
meaning of the words Calvinism and Calvinist. 'I use the
words Calvinism and Calvinist merely in compliance with
custom. The doctrinal system, established in England, which
Luther and Calvin were the honoured instruments of
retrieving, subsisted, from the beginning, in the faith of God's
elect people, and in the sacred Scriptures.'[7] In other words,
Calvinism aims to be simply the pure Christianity of the
Bible.

After an introduction relating the circumstances which led
to the writing of his book, Toplady proves the Calvinism of
King Edward VI and the Arminianism of the Church of
Rome. He claims the unanimous support of the writers of the
first four centuries, except the Arians, for the Calvinistic side
in the controversy with Arminians, and also the support of
very many other eminent Christians before the Reformation,
including Wyclif and Huss. The early English martyrs of the
Reformation, such as Bilney and Tyndale, also held the same
doctrines as Calvin.

Toplady deals next with the doctrines of our English
Reformers, in particular Cranmer, Ridley, Latimer, Hooper,
Bucer and Peter Martyr. He prefaces this section with these
words:

Very little need be said, to prove the Calvinism of those
illuminated divines, who were made, by Providence, the
instruments of extending and fixing the English
Reformation. The whole series of our public service, the
uniform tenor of our articles, and the chain of doctrine
asserted in each Book of Homilies, are a standing
demonstration, that the original framers and compilers
believed in, and worshipped, the God of their fathers, after
that way which Papists and Arminians term heresy.[8]

Toplady asks whether any but Calvinists would have drawn
up such statements as Articles IX to XVIII. In his book *The
Church of England Vindicated from the Charge of*

Arminianism he says: 'Open the liturgy where you will, Calvinism stares you in the face.'[9]

In the reign of Queen Mary Archbishop Cranmer offered 'to defend, not only the common prayers of the church, the ministration of the Sacraments, and other rites and ceremonies, but also all the doctrine and religion set out by our sovereign lord, king Edward VI., to be more pure and according to God's word than any other that hath been used in England these thousand years.'[10] Included in the doctrine of the time of Edward VI was Bishop Ponet's Catechism (otherwise known as King Edward's Catechism or Dr. Alexander Nowell's Catechism). This catechism was a kind of commentary on the Articles and contained the following statements:

As many as are in this faith stedfast, were fore-chosen, predestinated, and appointed to everlasting life, before the world was made. Witness hereof, they have within their hearts the spirit of Christ, the author, earnest, and unfailable pledge of their faith. Which faith only is able to perceive the mysteries of God; only brings peace unto the heart; only taketh hold on the righteousness which is in Christ Jesus.

...faith, or rather trust, alone, doth lay hand upon, understand, and perceive our righteous-making to be given us of God freely, that is to say, by no deserts of our own, but by the free grace of the Almighty Father....

By this short tale it is evident, whence, and by what means we attained to be righteous. For, not by the worthiness of our deservings, were we either heretofore chosen, or long ago saved; but by the only mercy of God, and pure grace of Christ our Lord: whereby we were, in him, made to do these good works, that God had appointed for us to walk in. And although good works cannot deserve to make us righteous before God, yet do they so cleave unto faith, that neither faith can be found without them, nor good works be any where found without faith....

Moreover, nature is so depraved and cast down, that unless the goodness and mercy of Almighty God had helped us by the medicine of grace, as in body we are thrust down into all the miseries of death, so it was necessary that all men of all sorts should be cast into eternal torments, and fire which cannot be quenched.[11]

This is some of the Biblical doctrine which King Edward VI commanded to be taught in all schools, and which was meant to be learnt by all Christians.

Cranmer himself subscribed to this catechism, and Toplady says: 'We must, therefore, admit, either that Cranmer was as absolute a predestinarian as Calvin himself; or charge the venerable archbishop with such extreme dissimulation and hypocrisy, as are utterly incompatible with common honesty. For, this catechism ... asserted the doctrines of predestination, efficacious grace, free justification, and final perseverance, in the fullest, strongest, and most explicit terms.'[12]

Bishop Latimer assisted Archbishop Cranmer in composing the Homilies which were published in 1547. Toplady says: 'Let any man but read them; and then doubt if he can, whether the composers were not Calvinist.'[13] Latimer was famous as a preacher, and his own sermons show his Calvinism.

> When we believe in him [Christ], it is like as if we had no sins. For he changeth with us; he taketh our sins and wickedness from us, and giveth us his holiness, righteousness, justice, fulfilling of the law; and so, consequently, everlasting life. So that we be like as if we had done no sin at all. For his righteousness standeth us in so good stead, as though we of ourselves had fulfilled the law to the uttermost.[14]

> The law, of itself, is holy and good. But we are not able to keep it; and therefore we must seek our righteousness, not in the law, but in Christ, who hath fulfilled the same, and given us freely his fulfilling.[15]

In 1547-8 King Edward VI and Archbishop Cranmer invited Peter Martyr, an Italian, to be Divinity professor at Oxford and Martin Bucer from Strasburg to be Divinity professor at Cambridge. Both these men helped in the English Reformation in addition to their work among students for the ministry of the Church of England. The newly-composed services were submitted for correction to these men who were convinced Calvinists. Even Calvin himself had a share in the Reformation of the Church of England through his correspondence with Cranmer and King Edward VI and the Duke of Somerset, who was the king's uncle and protector of the realm. Calvin gave advice about discontinuing prayers for the dead, the use of chrism, and extreme unction, since they are not to be found in the Bible, and about making worship more simple, as it was among European Protestants. Calvin was so esteemed at the English court that Bucer on his arrival in England would not present himself to the lord protector until he had letters of introduction from Calvin. Toplady is confident that no creditable writer in the Church of England spoke against Calvin until the time of Arminius.

Next Toplady lists his different proofs of the doctrinal Calvinism of the Church of England in the time of Queen Elizabeth. His most impressive proofs are selected for this paper out of the twenty he lists.

1. There was only one commentary on the Thirty-nine Articles published in the reign of Queen Elizabeth, that by Thomas Rogers. He dedicated his book to Archbishop Whitgift. In 1607 Rogers dedicated another edition to Archbishop Bancroft. Here is proof that the doctrine of the Church of England is Calvinistic, when the official commentary on the Articles dedicated to two Archbishops of Canterbury and approved by them is thoroughly Calvinistic in tone.

2. The marginal notes in the three Bibles published in the reign of Queen Elizabeth and with her sanction all follow the doctrines of Calvin. They were the Great Bible, the Bishops' Bible, and the Quarto Bible for the use of families. The Quarto Bible was first published in 1576, and again in 1582 and 1602. A marginal note on John 10: 26 ('Ye believe not, because ye are not of my sheep') reads: 'The cause wherefore the reprobate cannot believe.'[16] In the preface to the Epistle to the Romans the leaders of the Church of England wrote: 'The cause whereof is the only will of God; forasmuch of his free mercy, he electeth some to be saved, and of his just judgment, rejecteth others to be damned; as appeareth by the testimony of the Scriptures.'[17]

3. Questions and answers concerning predestination were inserted into authorised Bibles at least until 1614. They show that the doctrines of Calvin were the official view of the Church of England.

Quest. How standeth it with God's justice, that some are appointed unto damnation.

Answ. Very well: because all men have in themselves sin, which deserveth no less. And therefore the mercy of God is wonderful, in that he vouchsafeth to save some of that sinful race and to bring them to the knowledge of the truth....

Quest. But how shall I know myself to be one of those whom God hath ordained to life eternal?

Answ. By the motions of spiritual life, which belong only to the children of God: by the which, that life is perceived, even as the life of this body is discerned by the sense and motions thereof.

Quest. What mean you by the motions of spiritual life?

Answ. I mean remorse of conscience, joined with the lothing of sin, and love of righteousness; the hand of faith reaching unto life eternal in Christ; the conscience comforted in distress, and raised up to confidence in God, by the work of his Spirit; a thankful remembrance of God's benefits received; and the using of all adversities as occasion of amendment sent from God.

Quest. Cannot such perish, as at some time or other feel these motions within themselves?

Answ. It is not possible that they should: for, as God's purpose is not changeable, so he repenteth not of the gifts and graces of his adoption; neither doth he cast off those whom he hath once received.[18]

4. In 1566 the larger Helvetic Confession was drawn up. This Confession is thoroughly Calvinistic, and was approved by the Church of England, as it was by the Church of Scotland, the Reformed churches in France, and all the Dutch churches, together with many of the Protestant churches in Poland, Hungary, and Germany. Edmund Grindal, Bishop of London at this time, and afterwards Archbishop of Canterbury, writes to Henry Bullinger that 'down to this very day, we do perfectly agree with your churches, and with your confession of faith lately set forth.'[19]

5. It was not until 1595 that Calvinism was publicly attacked. Peter Baro of France was a refugee in Cambridge, and began to preach against predestination, together with William Barrett and Harsenet. Peter Heylyn, the historian, says they were the first Protestant divines since the Reformation publicly to attack the Calvinistic system. As a result Archbishop Whitgift and other bishops and divines produced the Lambeth Articles in which the Calvinistic doctrines of predestination, election and other controversial points are strongly asserted. Scholars in the universities had

to conform to these nine articles.

1. God hath, from eternity, predestinated certain persons to life; and hath reprobated certain persons unto death. 2. The moving, or efficient cause of predestination unto life, is not the foresight of faith, or of perseverance, or of good works, or of any thing that is in the persons predestinated: but the alone will of God's good pleasure. 3. The predestinate are a pre-determined and certain number, which can neither be lessened, nor increased. 4. Such as are not predestinated to salvation shall inevitably be condemned on account of their sins.... 8. No man is able to come to Christ, unless it be given him, and unless the Father draw him: and all men are not drawn by the Father, that they may come to his Son.

This Archbishop of Canterbury says of these Articles: 'I know them to be sound doctrines, and uniformly professed in this Church of England, and agreeable to the articles of religion established by authority.'[20]

6. During Queen Elizabeth's reign Dr. Willett's book *A General View of Papistry* was published. It was dedicated to the Queen and published by authority. Dr. Willett charges the Church of Rome with no fewer than 1,500 heresies and errors, and claims his Calvinistic faith to be that of the Queen and of the Church of England. On limited redemption he writes:

Here we are to consider the beginning of election, the progress thereof, and the end. The beginning: in that God, according to his good pleasure elected his, in Christ, before the foundation of the world. The progress: in that he hath given the elect unto Christ, to be saved and redeemed by him. The end is, that he hath purposed to bring them unto glory. Christ only was given to die for the company of the elect. Not that it is not sufficient for the whole world, in itself; but because the efficacy and benefit of Christ's death is only applied by faith to believers; and faith only is of the elect. Christ died, only for those that should believe in him. But it is not given to all, to believe in Christ, except only to the elect which are ordained to life. *Ergo*, for them only Christ died.[21]

7. The last proof brought by Toplady of the Calvinism of the Church of England under Queen Elizabeth is the fact that an order was issued for the placing of John Foxe's Calvinistic *Book of Martyrs* in all the parish churches of England for the people to read. A canon of 1571 also ordered this book to be

placed in all bishops' and church dignitaries' houses.

Toplady next reviews the situation in the Church of England after the death of Queen Elizabeth. For many years after King James I came to the throne in 1603 there was no change in the theology of the Archbishops and Bishops. The King himself was a Calvinist in theory, even if his life did not match his professed beliefs. Fifteen years after his accession to the crown of England, James I and the Church of England gave public proof of their continued Calvinism by the part they played in the work of the Synod of Dort in 1618-19. The Dutch took care to invite to their assistance in meeting the errors of the followers of Arminius only representatives from Calvinistic churches, such as the Church of England. The five representatives from England testified their full agreement with the Dutch confession of faith so far as doctrine was concerned. This was as strong a proof as they could give that they believed the teachings of Calvin. While at Dort they wrote to the Archbishop of Canterbury as follows, all signing the letter:

Nor do we, with the remonstrants, leave at large the benefit of our Saviour's death, as only propounded loosely to all, *ex aequo*, and to be applied by the arbitrary act of man's will; but we expressly avouch for the behoof of the elect, a special intention both in Christ's offering, and God the Father accepting: and, from that intention, a particular application of that sacrifice, by conferring faith, and other gifts, infallibly bring the elect to salvation.[22]

As he draws to his conclusion Toplady again briefly reviews the situation in the Church of England after the Reformation. He gives the testimony of Roman Catholic writers to the state of things. Scultingius says: 'In England Calvin's Book of Institutions is almost preferred to the Bible itself. The pretended English bishops enjoin all the clergy to get the book almost by heart, never to have it out of their hands, to lay it by them in a conspicuous part of their pulpits; in a word, to prize and keep it as carefully, as the old Romans are said to have preserved the Sybilline Oracles.'[23] Toplady says that the doctrinal Calvinism of Queen Elizabeth's bishops is almost incapable of exaggeration.

Even in the reign of Charles II there is the witness of Bishop Saunderson: 'When I began to set myself to the study of divinity as my proper business, Calvin's Institutions were recommended to me, as they were generally to all young scholars in those times, as the best and perfectest system of divinity, and the fittest to be laid as a groundwork of that profession. And indeed my expectation was not at all deceived, in the reading of those Institutions.'[24]

In the universities Calvinism reigned supreme during the reign of Queen Elizabeth. Heylyn cannot find a single instance of public opposition to Calvin's doctrines. In the middle of the reign of King James I he can only find two anti-Calvinists in the whole University of Oxford. In 1628 Dr. Samuel Ward of Cambridge University is able to report to Archbishop Usher: 'As for our University, none do patronise these (*i.e.* the Arminian) points, either in schools, or pulpit.'[25] In 1634 an Arminian clergyman was refused his degree by the majority vote of the Cambridge doctors, on the ground that he was an Arminian, although he was backed by people in power.

In conclusion Toplady mourns the dreadful declension of the majority of the members of the Church of England from the Scripture and the Church, in other words from Calvinism. He says:

> Our liturgy, our articles and our homilies, it is true, still keep possession of our church-walls: but we pray, we subscribe, we assent one way; we believe, we preach, we write another. In the desk, we are verbal Calvinists: but no sooner do we ascend a few steps above the desk, than we forget the grave character in which we appeared below, and tag the performance with a few minutes' entertainment compiled from the fragments bequeathed to us by Pelagius and Arminius; not to say by Arius, Socinus, and by others still worse than they.[26]

The only solution for Toplady and for us today is for the nominal members of our Church of England once again to become through the Holy Spirit real believers of its doctrines, which are the doctrines of the Bible and of Calvinism.

IV. FROM LAUD TO WATERLAND

The Rev. P.H. Buss, M.A.
Vicar of Christ Church, Fulham

A Momentous Century

The century from 1611 to 1711 (the reasons for this apparently
arbitrary choice of dates will become clearer anon) was a
momentous century. It was certainly so for *monarchs*. The
sixth James of Scotland had come south to claim his southern
inheritance. His son in turn was to lose his head and become
for many Charles King *and* Martyr. The Civil War took place,
the last such on English soil. The Commonwealth lived but a
short time — before by invitation and popular acclamation —
Charles II was restored to the throne, and the Stuarts
continued *pro tempore*. This was all to be lost by the ill-fated
attempts to re-establish Roman Catholicism by James II and
yet another invitation, this time to the Dutch Calvinist
William of Orange and his wife Mary to be the new King and
Queen. The Protestant Succession was written into the
English Constitution and it is there to this day, no small
testimony to the goings on of the seventeenth century: to say
nothing of the more strongly established position of
Parliament and the infant powers of democracy.

It was momentous *ecclesiastically*. Under Elizabeth
extreme Puritans were restrained, and so were Roman
Catholics. Whitgift and later Bancroft were no friends to
those who would not conform. Abbot, much maligned for his
lack of pressure upon Puritans but a good man in many ways,
gave way to Laud, who acted as Charles I's 'hatchet man'
against Nonconformists. Three great conferences took place
in this era: the Hampton Court Conference (1604), the
Westminster Assembly (1643-6), and the Savoy Conference
(1661). The first led to one abiding feature, the Authorized or
King James Version of the Bible. The second led to the

formulation of doctrine accepted as normative and fundamental by generations of Presbyterians. The third led to the '1662' Book of Common Prayer (basically the old 1552 Book but with additions mostly of minor import) and Ordinal, to which the Thirty-nine Articles are customarily appended. The importance of this for later evangelicals can be scarcely overestimated.

It was momentous for *ministries*. Two Archbishops of Canterbury incurred ominous charges and one, Sancroft, became a non-juror, because he could not swear allegiance to William, thus leading to suspension and deprivation. George Abbot in 1622, not renowned for accuracy with the cross bow, accidentally killed Peter Hawkins, a deerkeeper on Lord Zouch's estate at Bramshill. Protected by James I, he was shunned by Charles I, who increasingly found Laud a right-hand man in State and Church. Laud in turn was to be tried for treason (1641) during the Long Parliament, imprisoned, and executed in January 1645.

It was a momentous century for either *ejection* or *exodus* from the Church of England. The Puritans had greeted James I with the Millenary Petition. Signed by a hundred or two less than the thousand implied it was a concerted attempt by Puritans to reform the Church further after the Continental Reformers. Neither James nor Bancroft were in any mood to make concessions and the 1604 Canons were published, subscription enforced, and around three hundred clergy expelled from their livings. Nor should evangelicals gloss over the number of clergy in 1644 who could not subscribe to the Solemn League and Covenant. Over two thousand lost their livings. In 1662 when the boot was on the other foot, nearly two thousand clergy who could not accept episcopal re-ordination, and the Book of Common Prayer and Act of Uniformity, at St. Bartholomew's tide, were removed from their office: the so called 'Great Ejection'. There must also be borne in mind the many godly men who had left these shores, notably the Pilgrim Fathers on board the *Mayflower* in September 1620; they opened up the way for a massive emigration of Puritans to the New World, thus ensuring a considerable Protestant foothold on that continent. Last but not least must be included the non-jurors in 1689-90, headed by Sancroft, six bishops including Thomas Ken of Bath and Wells, and some four hundred clergy. It might well be posed how much a Church could afford to be bled so profusely and regularly and still retain vitality and health. By no means were all these men ones who could be included in an evangelical 'round up' but very many were.

The Evangelical Succession
The verdict must be given that, after the heyday of the Puritan influence in Elizabeth's reign and under James I, that influence was at first contained, and the more zealous and radical members removed, and then greatly reduced. Organised Nonconformity was about to emerge. By 1609 John Smyth and his exiled flock at Amsterdam had made believer's baptism the basis of Church fellowship. Next Thomas Helwys returned to England and in 1612 formed the first Baptist church at Spitalfields. By 1660 there were between two hundred and three hundred churches mostly in London and the South-East but also in the Midlands. There were also those who wanted to establish Presbyterian church government, and those who rejected any notion of a national church. So Independent/Congregational churches came into being, and also Presbyterian churches; to be followed by Quakers, who have survived to this day, and weirder sects who have long since vanished.

By 1611 it was clear that, barring a miracle, the powers that be had decreed that the Church of England was sufficiently reformed. This was the year the Authorized Version was published, the year Abbot became Primate, and the year Laud became President of St. John's College, Oxford, the college of his student days. Just over one hundred years later (1714) Waterland became the Master of the College of his student days, Magdalene College, Cambridge. These are useful book ends for the period, by no means cast-iron, not even wooden, but profitable to keep the information together.

To speak of the evangelical succession from the time of William Laud (1573-1645) to that of Daniel Waterland (1683-1740) is to use unfamiliar but not inaccurate language. The word 'evangelical' appears almost exclusively as an adjective meaning 'of the evangel' or 'of the gospel' in the literature of the seventeenth century, as it does in the sixteenth century. It does not appear to be generally attached to people until the eighteenth century. In this sense therefore G.R. Balleine was right to start his book on *A History of the*

Evangelical Party in the Church of England (1908) with that later period. The movement which changed the face of England in the second half of the eighteenth century was described with justification as the 'Evangelical Revival'. Balleine in a footnote shows the antiquity of the word 'evangelical'. He writes:

> It had been the earliest word in English for adherents of the Reformation, e.g. 'Those Evaungelicalles theimself cease not to pursue and punishe their bretherne' (Sir T. More, 1531).[1]

It is a pity that the word did not stick, but jostling with other epithets, Lollard, Lutherans, Protestants, it had to wait two hundred years before it found an agreed and established place in the English Church vocabulary. If any word is to include those of evangelical persuasion in the period under review it will be contained within the word 'Puritan'. As Balleine begins his work, 'Evangelical Churchmen trace their pedigree to the Puritans, the Reformers, and the Lollards, to all within the National Church who have learned to love a simple worship and a spiritual religion.'[2] If the name is not found at all frequently, the adjective is and certainly the people are.

V.H.H. Green in his book *Religion at Oxford and Cambridge*, a veritable mine of fascinating information, has the following quotation about an incident during the Commonwealth period at Oxford.

> Although Anglican services were proscribed, Dean Owen [that is John Owen of Christ Church and Vice-Chancellor of the University — a leading independent, and notable theologian] so his biographer averred,

> > suffered to meet quietly about three hundred *Evangelicals* according to the worship of the Church of England. And though he was often urged to it, yet he would never give them the least disturbance; and if any time they met with opposition or trouble on that account it was from other hands and always against his mind.

This meeting, on Sundays and week-days, took place at the lodgings of Mr. T. Willis, the physician, in Canterbury Quadrangle or later at his home

> against Merton College church, to which place admitting none but their confidants, prayers and surplices were used on all Lord's Days, Holy Days and their Vigils, as

also the Sacrament according to the Church of England administered.

There was then some opportunity, albeit at peril, for loyal Anglicans to take part in the worship of the proscribed Prayer Book.[3]

Here is a fascinating note. Evangelicals are clearly here Anglican evangelicals. One would dearly like to know more about them.

Bishop J.C. Ryle described an evangelical religion as that which has the following features: (a) the absolute supremacy it assigns to Holy Scripture; (b) the depth and prominence it assigns to the doctrine of human sinfulness and corruption; (c) the paramount importance it attaches to the work and office of our Lord Jesus Christ; (d) the high place it assigns to the inward work of the Holy Spirit in the heart of man; (e) the importance which it attaches to the outward and visible work of the Holy Ghost in the life of man. Evangelical religion, he goes on, does *not* despise learning, research or the wisdom of days gone by, does *not* undervalue the church, nor the Christian ministry nor the sacraments of baptism and the Lord's supper, nor the Prayer Book, nor episcopacy, nor handsome churches, nor Christian unity, nor Christian holiness nor self denial.[4] John Stott in simpler vein describes evangelicals as 'Bible people and Gospel people'.[5] These are the men that it is necessary to look for in the hundred years or so between 1611 and 1711. And these men can be found in the Church of England as reformed but also outside.

Changes in Worship
First of all it will be more helpful to describe visible changes in fabric and worship, because these are tangible and observable to people.

For the ordinary person the changes that came over Church life would be nowhere more obvious than at his local place of worship. If a typical country church were visited in the year 1511, certain features would be standard. The service was in Latin, barely audible to the congregation. They would not be particularly involved apart from certain bowings and crossings. They would not communicate at Mass except at Easter. The font lay at its time-honoured place at the west end of the church near the entrance porch. The pulpit, if there was one, would not be a conspicuous item because sermons were rare. There were sermons all round the church walls, as long as they were continuously interpreted — great murals of Judgement, Heaven, and Hell. If it was a rich, well-endowed church, there might be stained glass windows and some paving on the floor. A few benches were there for the convenience of the elderly. Candles flickered, the incense arose, and many painted statues overlooked the scene. It was a colourful, mysterious, awesome place. The priest surrounded by his servers and acolytes was at the altar offering the Mass, repeating the sacrifice of Christ for the living and the dead. A professional man of God was doing something an ordinary mortal could never do. Salvation was by belonging to the Church and doing what the Church said, keeping within its orbit, not by private thinking and action. Doubtless dire notices were given out to the faithful warning them of the eternal perils of heresy. Perhaps there were a handful in the village tainted with Lollardy. In that very year they could have heard of one Thomas Man who was imprisoned by Bishop Smyth of Lincoln for denying transubstantiation, auricular confession, extreme unction, and image worship. Certainly in the vast diocese of Lincoln which included the Chilterns and stretched down to the Thames there would be tiny congregations, and travelling preachers and teachers, preparing the way for the Reformation; reverencing the Wycliffe Bible and persevering in a nonconformity in some places with great heroism.

Using the reconstruction provided by Professor Owen Chadwick the scene shifts one hundred years:

A Protestant minister, standing in his English pulpit about the year 1600, would find much similar to the old church — the stone stoup to the side of the door, the font in its old place, the open nave with stools and a few benches, the men still sitting on one side and the women on the other, the magnate's pew (somewhat enlarged now; there were perhaps one or two new private pews), the floor strewn with rushes and straw, for this village vestry had not yet been able to afford what was done in some other village churches, the covering of the floor of the church with flagstones. (As late as the eighteenth century there were some country churches with a bare floor.) One corner of the church might be a heap of earth, but he was used to men being buried inside the building. Some of the older people still bowed towards the altar on entry, though countrywomen mistook this for a curtsy to the minister. The church, in comparison with the same church seventy years before, would give him a sense of coolness, of absence of clutter, of bareness and nakedness. Though the oak screen still divided the chancel from the church, the rood loft above it had disappeared, the statues to the left and right likewise, the pictures which hung on the walls had been removed, and the frescoes which, in their newest glow, had given the body of the church a sense of rosiness and warmth, but in dilapidation distracted the mind and made the church seem tawdry, were concealed beneath a cool whitewash. The organ, if the old church had an organ, was not to be seen. He would probably have seen the Royal Arms, though their display was not compulsory by law, and the Ten Commandments inscribed upon the wall. The overwhelming impression must have been change from dark to light, cosiness to austerity, clutter to bareness. And how the soul responded would depend on its taste and temperament as well as its wont.[6]

To this picture can be added one or two more features. The Great Bible had its place of honour in the body of the church, but not to be read daily as in the first days of the Reformation, because people had their pocket Geneva Bibles and prayer at home. The worship of the church was much more congregational, and of course in English. There would have been a sermon quite regularly or a Homily read, and the young catechised. There might have been attached to the church by the local patron, especially if it was a thriving village, a Lecturer, even to the disapproval of the Rector. These were days when Puritanism was strong and the systematic exposition of God's word paramount. In the next village the Rector might have dispensed with the Prayer Book liturgy and composed his own, praying extempore, preaching at length and without a surplice. The work of the Reformers is clear, but tensions exist between the conservative evangelical reformers and their radical evangelical colleagues. As early as 1549 Sternhold had produced metrical versions of the psalms, nineteen in number. By 1562 the whole psalter was covered and in spite of some indifferent renderings this form of singing became very popular. By the end of Elizabeth's reign cathedrals and collegiate churches were using the music of Byrd, Gibbons, Morley, Tallis, and Weelkes, but this would not have percolated through to the ordinary church.

A further hundred years on, say to 1711, and the scene has changed again. The Communion Table has found its way back to the east end. Some people might call it an 'altar', and it has rails round it. Choir stalls may have been resurrected. Floors of the church are being paved, pews are more commonplace, pulpit balances lectern. Stained glass windows might have been added. There might be a cross and statues, as long as they were historical and not of saints. The Church of England has firmly rejected 'popery' but there are signs to make a good Puritan suspicious that everything gained in the sixteenth century had not lasted into the eighteenth century. The organ, much frowned upon in Puritan circles, might well have re-appeared or a gallery at the back with room for a handful of instrumentalists. Singing was still almost exclusively metrical psalms. In 1696 the version of Tate and Brady had been published and began to supersede Sternhold and Hopkins. Hymns from such diverse writers as Richard Baxter, Thomas Ken, and Isaac Watts were beginning to find favour and popularity. New churches had been built, especially after the Great Fire of London, by Wren and others and these were light, open, dignified churches designed essentially for preaching, the so-called 'auditory churches'. In the vast majority of country churches a feel of mediaevalism was around. It is a moot point how deep this feeling was and how prevalent. It could well be argued that in spite of the carriage of the Reformation principles into worship, doctrine, Bible knowledge, and living, there were still tracts of a collective subconscious untouched. Retouched by the Oxford Movement this still in the twentieth century confronts and confounds the space-age parson.   If the re-ordering is to be laid at the door of any man it must be that of William Laud. If the ostensible doctrinal orthodoxy, for the most part, of the Church of England in the eighteenth and early nineteenth century is to be apportioned, it can truly be done so to the massive scholarship of men like Daniel Waterland. More noticeable evidence, as far as the man in the pew was concerned, of the differing styles of Christianity would be the existence in the village of a Baptist Chapel, and in the neighbouring village of an Independent Chapel. While up at the big house it was well known that Roman Catholics

still met for their surreptitious mass. The Church in England
was no longer monolithic, either in its unreformed or reformed
status.

It is very much the seventeenth century, the period from
Laud to Waterland, that has seen the crystallisation of this
situation. The Church of England is the established Church.
The Nonconformists have gained a foothold in the national
life. The tiny Roman Catholic minority has been cast into the
wilderness. Presbyterianism has been tried and found
wanting in the English climate, though it survives
tenaciously in Scotland. Interestingly the Church of Scotland
today has a larger proportion of the population than any
other Protestant Church in the English-speaking world. It
was essentially a century of strong, and even bitter, feelings
that only in this century seem to be dying down. Even today
there are some Anglicans who find it hard to think of the
'chapel' as a 'church': some Free Churchmen who find it hard
to accept that there are real believers in the established
Church.

The People and the Book
Later research has modified J. Richard Green's memorable
verdict on the later Elizabethan and the Jacobean era. But he
deserves to be heard again:

No greater moral change ever passed over a nation than
passed over England during the years which parted the
middle of the reign of Elizabeth from the meeting of the
Long Parliament. England became the people of a book,
and that book was the Bible. It was as yet the one English
book which was familiar to every Englishman; it was read
at churches and read at home, and everywhere its words, as
they fell on ears which custom had not deadened, kindled a
startling enthusiasm....

The whole prose literature of England, save the forgotten
tracts of Wyclif, has grown up since the translation of the
Scriptures by Tyndale and Coverdale. So far as the nation
at large was concerned, no history, no romance, hardly any
poetry, save the little-known verse of Chaucer, existed in
the English tongue when the Bible was ordered to be set up
in churches. Sunday after Sunday, day after day, the
crowds that gathered round Bonner's Bibles in the nave of
St. Paul's, or the family group that hung on the words of the

Geneva Bible in the devotional exercises at home, were
leavened with a new literature....

But far greater than its effect on literature or social
phrase was the effect of the Bible on the character of the
people at large. Elizabeth might silence or tune the pulpits;
but it was impossible for her to silence or tune the great
preachers of justice, and mercy, and truth, who spoke from
the book which she had again opened for her people. The
whole moral effect which is produced now-a-days by the
religious newspaper, the tract, the essay, the lecture, the
missionary report, the sermon, was then produced by the
Bible alone; and its effect in this way, however
dispassionately we examine it, was simply amazing. One
dominant influence told on human action: and all the
activities that had been called into life by the age that was
passing away were seized, concentrated, and steadied to a
definite aim by the spirit of religion. The whole temper of
the nation felt the change. A new conception of life and of
man superseded the old. A new moral and religious impulse
spread through every class. Literature reflected the general
tendency of the time; and the dumpy little quartos of
controversy and piety, which still crowd our older libraries,
drove before them the classical translations and Italian
novelettes of the age of the Renascence. 'Theology rules
there' said Grotius of England only two years after
Elizabeth's death; and when Casaubon, the last of the great
scholars of the sixteenth century, was invited to England
by King James, he found both King and people indifferent
to pure letters. 'There is a great abundance of theologians
in England', he says, 'all point their studies in that
direction'.[7]

The Geneva Bible had been produced by Protestant exiles,
probably including William Whittingham and John Knox.
The cost was defrayed by members of the Geneva
congregation 'whose hearts God had touched' to encourage
the revisers not to spare any effort in such an enterprise. John
Bodley, the father of the founder of the Bodleian Library, was
much involved. In a modest quarto size, printed in Roman
lettering, showing the chapters divided into verses, and with
comments slightly tinged with Calvinism, this version, not
surprisingly, became the household Bible of the
English-speaking nations, and it continued to be so for

seventy-five years. It is estimated that between 1560 and 1644 at least one hundred and forty editions of the Genevan Bible or Testament appeared.

Following the Hampton Court Conference translators were appointed to produce an acceptable revision of the Bible. The names of the men making up the six companies employed on the work have come down to us, and with one or two exceptions — the irascible Hugh Broughton, the greatest Hebrew scholar of the day, was omitted — they were the best men available. Their progress through the work is little recorded. When their version appeared it became known as the 'Authorized Version', although it is very hard, if not impossible, to discover either royal or ecclesiastical sanction. The Biblical chaos that followed was not unlike that of the present day. Five editions of the A.V. followed in three years. Eight editions of the Bishops' New Testament were printed by the King's Printers in the next eight years. Thirteen editions of the Genevan Bible or Testament appeared between 1611 and 1617. Gradually the A.V. won the day earning the ascription from Brian Walton (1600-1661), Bishop of Chester, and compiler of the great 'Polyglot Bible', 'Inter omnes eminet'. It must be acknowledged that the pioneering work of William Tyndale amounts to a considerable percentage of the work and that this version has for three hundred years been *the* version of the English-speaking world. Indeed it is for some the hallmark of evangelical orthodoxy to use the A.V. over against all the modern versions.

If the publishing and buying of Bibles is anything to go by there is good evidence to support Green's thesis. Considering, too, the preciousness of books and the sheer exuberance with which people came to the Bible, such days were halcyon days and days where there was every opportunity to be a Bible person. These were days too of great preaching. Thomas Goodwin rode over from Christ's College, Cambridge, to hear John Rogers preach at Dedham. Described as one of the most awakening of preachers of his day Bishop Brownrigge used to say 'he did more good with his wild Notes than we [the Bishops] with our set Musick'. One is reminded of the Archbishop of York's retort to those who criticised mad Grimshaw of Haworth in the next century.

It was the era too of Biblical commentaries. Henry

Ainsworth on the Pentateuch (1616), George Hughes on Genesis (1672), Philip Henry (1631-1696) (father of the great Matthew Henry) on Genesis 1-11, Richard Rogers on Judges (1615). There was the work of Daniel Rogers on Naaman (1642 — 898 folio pages) — 'large enough to have loaded one of Naaman's mules' (C.H. Spurgeon) — to vie with Joseph Caryl's epic on Job, 12 volumes quarto (1643-1666) and John Collinges' exposition on the Song of Solomon (1676 — 909 quarto pages on chapter 1 and 530 on chapter 2). Edward Reynolds, Bishop of Norwich, wrote a much valued commentary on Psalm 110 (1632). Nor was the New Testament neglected. John Boys (1571-1625), Dean of Canterbury, wrote a commentary on the Epistles and Gospels (1610). Bishop John Davenant of Salisbury wrote a memorable commentary on Colossians (1627), William Gouge on Hebrews (1655), and John Owen on the same book (1668-74).

Put alongside these the massive works of theology like John Owen on the Holy Spirit (1674), Stephen Charnock on the 'existence and attributes of God'; add the more devotional works like Richard Baxter's *The Saints' Everlasting Rest* (1650) and Richard Sibbes' *The Bruised Reed* (1630) and the matchless *The Pilgrim's Progress* (1678) of John Bunyan, and his *Grace Abounding to the chief of Sinners* (1666); and for final measure the sermons of Thomas Watson, Thomas Manton, and Edmund Calamy, to select but a few, and the sum is a mighty one.

At the beginning of the last quarter of the seventeenth century men began to band together against the dissoluteness of the times and form 'Societies'. The aim of the societies was the promotion of holiness of life, to be a regular worshipper in the Church of England, and to be pleasant to Dissenters, to meet once a week for mutual encouragement and Bible Study and to avoid worldly or contentious matters. Each member was to introduce a further member. Dr. Anthony Horneck of the Savoy Chapel provided the inspiration; Smythies of St. Michael Cornhill helped, and supporters numbered William Beveridge the Vicar of St. Peter Cornhill, later Bishop of St. Asaph and author of a book on the Thirty-nine Articles, and Thomas Tenison of St. Martin-in-the-Fields, who was to become Archbishop of Canterbury. By 1698 there were thirty-two groups in London and they had spread as far as

Dublin. In 1691 the Society for the Reformation of Manners was formed to influence public morality for good. The Society for the Promotion of Christian Knowledge had been started by Dr. Thomas Bray (1656-1730) in 1698. In 1701 Bray had won the support of Tenison and the Society for the Propagation of the Gospel in Foreign Parts was launched. In the reign of Queen Anne many of these societies were caught up in the High Church movement. But there is a direct line with the Evangelical Revival. Samuel Wesley, in his parish at Epworth, had one such society and they were still going strong when Whitefield visited London.

Societies for Bible study, Christian fellowship, encouragement to regular worship, sermons, Bible commentaries, and Bibles; societies to spread the faith, to reform manners, to increase Christian education and knowledge: amidst all the wear and tear, the rough and tumble of the century there is much to be said for the thesis that Churchmen and Chapelmen were men of the Bible. The Bible was probably more deeply studied by all shades of opinion, both devotionally and academically than for a long, long while afterwards. The marks of evangelical religion that Ryle noted would be marked by most men. The categories of importance would be agreed. That there was a wider agreement about the basis of the faith then than there is today is indisputable.

Dark Corners
But there were still dark corners to be visited with the light of the gospel. In his dedicatory epistle 'To the right worshipful and well-beloved, the Parishioners of St. Clement's, Eastcheap' before his famous *An Exposition of the Creed* (first edition, 1659), John Pearson, Bishop of Chester (died 1686), wrote:

> The principles of Christianity are now as freely questioned as the most doubtful and controverted points; the grounds of faith are as safely denied as the most unnecessary superstructions; that religion hath the greatest advantage which appeareth in the newest dress, whereas in Christianity there can be no concerning truth which is not ancient; and whatsoever is truly new, is certainly false.[8]

Right in London Pearson had cause for complaint. What about the further corners of the realm?

Way back in 1551 itinerant ministers had been appointed to go in circuit round Wales, Lancashire, Yorkshire, the Scottish Borders, Devon, and Hampshire; only limited success was reported, and it was these regions which proved such a problem to the central government and such a source of hope to the Papacy. The borders of Wales, that principality, and the Scottish borders gave special cause for concern. Preaching was rare to the point of being phenomenal in many areas. Bishops in their visitations produced lamentable statistics. In some cases Puritan preachers who had outworn their welcome in London and the Home Counties were sent to tougher areas. At the Hampton Court Conference these ungospelled areas were discussed, and good preachers promised by the King himself, but nothing came of it. Evangelism promised but put into abeyance by the Church of England. Truly there is nothing new under the sun.

One of the great banes to a concerted evangelistic attempt was impropriation. The central funds were so short of cash that livings were constantly ransacked and a pittance given to a curate to hold the fort. Private enterprise made a shortlived but enlightened attempt to meet these spiritual needs. The Feoffees were made up of London merchants, lawyers, and ministers. They supported lecturers in Wales and its borders, and were suppressed by Laud in 1633 after eight years in operation. Christopher Hill in an essay on the 'Puritans and the Dark Corners of the Land' in his work *Change and Continuity in Seventeenth-Century England* describes how Laud put an end to these 'Gatherings of Londoners to discuss "how to set up the light of the gospel in the dark places of your county", "to set up weekly lectures ... in places most destitute of the gospel" '.[9] After 1640 they were resumed, London merchants banding together to support and work in the county of their origin.

Hill also quotes Charles I's approval for Laud's suppression of an itinerant lecturer in Lichfield and Coventry: 'If there be dark corners in that diocese, it were fit a true light should illuminate it; and not this that is false and uncertain.'[10] But no true light took its place: the corners remained dark.

With the advent of the Long Parliament, and without the episcopal brakes on, attention was once more directed to the neglected parts of the country. In 1650 a committee for the Propagation of the Gospel in Wales was formed and became a

real power in that land. The Bible newly translated into
Welsh was snapped up. There was also a Committee for the
North. In both areas schools were set up, free and some open
to boys and girls: 'The first provision for education ever made
by the State in Great Britain.'[11] In 1660 all but one school
ceased in Wales. The Baptists, Independents, and Quakers
moved in. As with Presbyterians in Scotland with a tiny
episcopal church, so Wales was won for Nonconformity with
the blessing of the bishops of the Church of England.

William Laud
It is time to turn to William Laud, whose presence looms over
this century and beyond. He was born in 1573. His family
were well-to-do traders in Reading. Brilliant at school, he
moved on to Oxford and to St. John's College, where he was
successively undergraduate, Lecturer, Tutor, and President.
The prevailing theology at Oxford was Calvinist — the most
influential man was George Abbot, Master of University
College. In 1604 for his B.D. thesis Laud maintained two
positions which caused great consternation and opposition:
first that baptism was necessary to salvation, and secondly
that there could be no true church without diocesan bishops.
Laud had thrown down the gauntlet bravely indeed, and
probably rashly, but also portentously. Involved in a wedding
ceremony of some notoriety, he spent a few years in country
livings before being called back to Oxford. In 1616 he became
Dean of Gloucester and one of his first acts was to remove the
communion table from the middle of the choir to the upper end
of the cathedral, meaning the east end. Dr. Miles Smith, the
Bishop of Gloucester, was so offended by the Dean's action
that he never again set foot in the Cathedral.

Laud had a passion for what he considered was proper. He
made sure with his successive promotions that each place was
put in order and due ceremony observed. He encouraged
people to bow on entering church and at the name of Jesus.
There is a striking example of the efficacy of Laud's
insistence on this act in a ministerial examination on
December 31, 1650. William Bagshawe, later to earn the title
'Apostle of the Peak', was examined by the Presbytery for the
Hundred of Scarsdale. Richard Maudsley of Dronfield asked:

Give your reply to the Laudian prelates whose excuse for
bowing their knees at the name of Jesus is that celebrated

text, Philippians 2: 10.

Bagshawe: I doubt not the word 'name' is in this text, as in divers others, to be construed not for the bare syllables thereof, for the mere word is not the object of faith or adoration; but, of Christ's name, we are to understand His person, as clothed with His power and authority. I doubt not, by bowing at or in His name is meant subjection to Him and worship of Him.[12]

So the practice — so the typical Puritan riposte.

In 1621 Laud became Bishop of St. David's. He was involved in a public controversy with the Jesuit Fisher, whose real name was Percy. The Counter-Reformation was well under way at this time, and this potent spearhead of Roman Catholic missionaries of the Society of Jesus something to be contended with. It is argued that Laud's efforts show conclusively that he was no Romaniser. In his letter of resignation as Chancellor of Oxford in 1641 Laud wrote: 'it is *vox populi* that I am popishly affected. How earnest I have been in my disputations, exhortations, and otherwise to quench such sparks, lest they should become coals, I hope after my death you will all acknowledge.'[13] The rest of his ecclesiastical career is well known. From Bath and Wells he passed to London, and thence in 1633 to Canterbury.

Laud will long be argued over. High Churchmen see him as the saviour of the catholicity and continuity of the Church, the lover of liturgy, the enforcer of uniformity, the protagonist for the beauty of holiness in worship. But even his admirers cannot evade the unhappy alliance between Charles I and himself. H.D.M. Spence wrote: 'The student of history reads with unfeigned amazement the pages of some of the archbishop's apologists here. Laud's work as a statesman may be wondered at, grieved over, but never can be excused.'[14] As a supporter to the hilt of the Divine Right of Kings and a relentless persecutor of Puritans he will be ever remembered. After the Restoration it was a Church of England much marked by Laudianism that was re-established.

Evangelicals see him as an opponent of the continuity of reform. The refusal on his part to accept a Cardinal's hat is seen as evidence not of his anti-Romanism but of his fitness to earn the offer in the first place. An angular character who had a vision for a future Church of England, he had little sympathy for his differing contemporaries and was an iconoclast reversed. The division between Reformed members of the Church of England and seceders was helped not a little by Laud. Laud was munificent to Oxford, and generous in supporting scholarship; yet it is noteworthy that, while Charles' death was soon considered by some a martyrdom, Laud's was not.

Behind Laud there was a group of distinguished men — the 'Caroline Divines', notably Lancelot Andrewes, John Cosin, Nicholas Ferrar, George Herbert, Thomas Fuller, Richard Montague and Jeremy Taylor. While acknowledging some of the gains of the Reformation, and often more moderate than Laud himself, they took great alarm at the fragmentation of Christendom. They went back through the mediaeval church to the primitive Church and the Early Fathers. Episcopacy was essential rather than beneficial — of the *esse* of the Church rather than the *bene esse*. The Communion service must be frequent and primary. The table, often called 'altar', must have the place of honour, the pulpit a secondary place. Stained-glass windows, crooks, even crucifixes reappeared. Prayers for the departed and the Holy Communion described in terms of 'eucharistic sacrifice' crept into the language and literature. Even a monasticism appeared at Little Gidding for eleven years. The *media via* which is such a glory of the Church of England (or such a nuisance!), the Carolines claimed, was between Rome and Geneva. There is in fact a lot more to be said: if there was a *media via* in the Church of England, historically speaking it was between Geneva and Wittenburg. But the Carolines have carried the popular day.

There will always be a conflict between the 'wilderness' mentality and the 'settlement' mentality. There will be always those for whom the glory of God is not enhanced by the efforts of men and for whom beauty is simplicity.

To call on the Name of God ... if men truly know and mean what they are doing, is in itself an act so tremendous and so full of comfort that any sensuous or artistic heightening of the effect is not so much a painting of the lily as a varnishing of the sunlight.[15]

This is the Puritan and indeed the evangelical position. There will always be on the other hand those who want to make their local church as Solomon's temple — 'exceeding magnifical' — for the glory of God. Laud's mistake was to

reintroduce and re-order furniture in the Stuart period that
the Reformers had extracted to remove all trace of uncatholic
Christian faith and order, thinking that men would reckon no
doctrinal change were implied. In those hectic days to hope to
conduct reformed worship in more or less Roman Catholic
surroundings was asking too much. John Cosin was to
reappear at the Restoration as one of the architects of the
revised Prayer Book. In the restoration period, as with James
I and Bancroft, short shrift was given to Puritan consciences
by Charles II, and John Sheldon, Bishop of London and then
Archbishop of Canterbury. August 24, 1662, has already been
referred to. It was not just the loss of individuals but the
expulsion of a party. The Church of England had to wait over
a hundred years before it had within its ranks even a
percentage of like-minded men for pastoral care, evangelistic
zeal, and Biblical ministries.

Some men of evangelical persuasion submitted to episcopal
re-ordination; one such was William Gurnall of Lavenham,
famous for his exposition of Ephesians 6, *The Christian in
complete armour* (1655-62). More were like Thomas Guage of
St. Sepulchre's, Holborn, who left the metropolis for Wales. By
1675 he had founded over fifty schools, and repaired some of
the Restoration damage to education. He helped with the
printing of the Welsh Bible, much aided by London friends.
Another evangelist to the Welsh was Hugh Owen.

Theological Trends
The years following 1660 were dismal for Nonconformists: the
Corporation Act (1661), the Act of Uniformity (1662), the
Conventicle Act (1664), the Five Mile Act (1666), and the Test
Act (1673) were all directed against them. The few Roman
Catholics in the country were sufferers of course, but this was
nothing compared with the harassing of the Free Church
men. Scotland went through times of harsh persecution, and
the courage of the Covenanters has become a legend. For the
Church of England evangelical the baptism by fire was the
sixteenth century, for the Nonconformist it was the
seventeenth.

It is sobering to note that the college in Cambridge which
had produced most Puritans, Emmanuel College, the
foundation of Walter Mildmay, produced in the middle of the
century the majority of the men known as 'Cambridge

Platonists': Ralph Cudworth, Nathaniel Culverwel, Henry More, John Smith, and Benjamin Whichcote. The mood of the movement was 'reasonableness'. Reason was the 'voice of God'. They reacted against the intensity of the long-lasting controversies and hoped that an appeal to reason would produce reasonable men. Dogmatic statements which divided men gave place to moral encouragement to inspire men. Philosophy and theology were to be reconciled at reason's bar. Much given to prayer and meditation they had a lasting impact through the men who followed them. These were the 'Latitudinarians'. Originally the Platonists had been called by this name, but by a quirk it was transferred to their successors, Simon Patrick, Bishop of Ely, Edward Stillingfleet, Bishop of Worcester, and two Archbishops of Canterbury, John Tillotson and Thomas Tenison. Even Moorman in his one-volume history of the Church of England, not notable for its Puritan sympathies, is moved to record 'that they lacked the humility and reverence of their masters and were more self-confident and assured.'[16] Extolling reason, they abominated enthusiasm.

It is interesting to compare the work of Bishop Gilbert Burnet of Salisbury on the Thirty-nine Articles (1699) with that of Beveridge of St. Asaph (published posthumously in 1710). Burnet breathes a spirit of reasonableness. On Article XI he wrote 'By *faith only,* is not to be meant faith as it is separated from the other evangelical graces and virtues; but faith, as it is opposite to the rites of the Mosaical law.'[17] Or on Article X, he wrote, 'The revelation of religion is the proposing and proving many truths of great importance to our understandings, by which they are enlightened, and our wills are guided .... The giving those truths of religion such a force that they may be able to subdue nature, and to govern us, is the design of both *natural* and revealed religion.'[18] In all this there is assent to the orthodox faith but a lack of real passion and commitment.

Now listen to the strength and clarity of Beveridge on Article XI:

A man is justified by faith only, and not by works; but a man that is justified cannot but have works also as well as faith. And as his person is justified by faith only before God, so is his faith justified by works only before men and his own conscience. It is by faith only, and not by works,

that a man is accounted righteous in heaven; but it is by
works only, and not by faith, that a man is esteemed
righteous upon earth. So that though a man be justified by
his faith that goes before, we do not know that he is justified
but only by his works that follow after....

What therefore, if I should fast my body into a skeleton,
and pray my tongue, and hear my ears, to their very
stumps? What though I should water my couch continually
with my tears, fasten my knees always to the earth by
prayer, and fix my eyes constantly into heaven by
meditation? What though I should give every thing I have
to my poor distressed neighbours, and spend each moment
of my time in the immediate worshipping of my glorious
Maker? Would any of this be more than I am bound to do?
Should not I still be an unprofitable servant? And if I can do
no more than is my duty unto God, how can I merit any
thing by what I do for him? How can he be indebted unto me
for my paying of what I owe to him?[19]

Reason is here, but Scripture is primary and forceful
argument. Compare them, too, on Article XVIII. First, Burnet:

Instead of stretching the severity of justice by an inference,
we may rather venture to stretch the mercy of God, since
that is the attribute which of all others is the most
magnificently spoken of in the scriptures: so that we ought
to think of it in the largest and most comprehensive
manner. But indeed the most proper way is, for us to stop
where the revelation of God stops; and not to be wise beyond
what is written; but to leave the secrets of God as mysteries
too far above us to examine, or to sound their depth. We do
certainly know on what terms we ourselves shall be saved
or damned: and we ought to be contented with that, and
rather study to *work out our own salvation with fear and
trembling,* than to let our minds run out into uncertain
speculations concerning the measures and the conditions of
God's uncovenanted mercies: we ought to take all possible
care that we ourselves come not into condemnation, rather
than to define positively of others, who must, or who must
not, be condemned.[20]

And then Beveridge:

So that let a man be never so strict a Jew, never so strict a
Mahumetan, never so strict in any other religion
whatsoever, unless he be a Christian he can never be saved.

So that though many Christians may go to hell, yet none
but Christians can ever go to heaven; many that profess
Christ may not be saved, yet all that deny Christ are certain
to be damned: for it is by Christ and Christ only, that we
can be saved.[21]

Daniel Waterland

Platonists begat Latitudinarians, and Latitudinarians begat
Deists. Deism began in earnest with Toland's *Christianity
not Mysterious* (1696), and reached a peak with Tindal's
Christianity as old as the Creation (1730). Butler's famous
Analogy put up the orthodox case in reply. Samuel Clarke in
1712 from his position of Rector of St. James, Piccadilly, wrote
The Scripture-Doctrine of the Trinity in which he denied the
orthodox teaching of the Trinity and the charge of Arianism
was levelled. Waterland answered the charges with great
solidity and strength in 1719 with his *A Vindication of
Christ's Divinity*. Just five years later his *A Critical History
of the Athanasian Creed* was published, which for 150 years
was standard reading on the subject.

Born in Lincolnshire in 1683, Waterland was educated at
Lincoln School and Magdalene College, Cambridge. In 1714
he became Master of his college — an office he held until 1740.
He was also a Canon of Windsor and Archdeacon of
Middlesex, from which office he gave four charges to the
clergy of Middlesex in 1736, 1738, 1739, and 1740 on the
Doctrine of the Eucharist. These are appended to a book
which gathered his teaching on that subject, which was
re-published in 1868 at the request of the then Archbishop of
Canterbury. In the Preface the Bishop of Lincoln of the time
wrote that this was 'a treatise which was considered almost
as the text book of the Church of England on the subject of the
Eucharist.'[22] Subsequent generations are indebted to the
massive and pacific scholarship of Waterland. On areas of
real contention, the Person of Christ, the wisdom of the
Church of England maintaining within its liturgy the
Athanasian Creed 'with its damnatory clauses', and the
Eucharist he needs to be heard again. Lesser men have had
books about them — it is time for Waterland to be reassessed.
He discusses all the words connected with the Eucharist. He
has a real understanding of the early Fathers and shows a
wide grasp of the Reformation writers, both English and

Continental. It is a rare treat to see Cranmer so well
understood, the teaching of the Prayer Book and Articles and
Homilies so clearly expounded, and an appreciation of the
formative writers on the Eucharist in the sixteenth century so
faithfully given. Let Waterland and then Cranmer be heard in
concert:

> Wherefore to avoid all such needless suppositions and
> needless perplexities, let us be content to teach only this
> plain doctrine; that we eat Christ crucified in this
> Sacrament, as we partake of the merits of his death: and if
> we thus have part in his crucified body, we are thereby ipso
> facto made partakers of the body glorified; that is we recive
> our Lord's body into a closer union than before, and become
> his members by repeated and stronger ties; provided we
> come worthily to the holy table, and that there is no just
> obstacle, on our part, to stop the current of Divine graces.

I may shut up this account with the excellent words of
Archbishop Cranmer, as follows, only put into the modern
spelling:

> The first Catholic Christian faith is most plain, clear, and
> comfortable, without any difficulty, scruple, or doubt:
> that is to say, that our Saviour Christ, although he be
> sitting in heaven, in equality with his Father, is our life,
> strength, food and sustenance; who by his death delivered
> us from death, and daily nourishes and increases us to
> eternal life. And in token hereof, he hath prepared bread
> to be eaten, and wine to be drunk of us in his holy Supper,
> to put us in remembrance of his said death, and of the
> celestial feeding, nourishing, increasing, and of all the
> benefits which we have thereby: which benefits, through
> faith and the Holy Ghost, are exhibited and given unto all
> that worthily receive the said holy Supper. This the
> husbandman at his plough, the weaver at his loom, and
> the wife at her rock, can remember, and give thanks unto
> God for the same: this is the very doctrine of the Gospel,
> with the consent wholly of all the old ecclesiastical
> doctors.'[23]

Adherence to Reformed Truth

It is sometimes imagined that many Anglicans in the
seventeenth century turned their back on the Reformers and
no longer adhered to their tenets. Richard Hooker wrote of the

Reformation as 'wonderfully marked by divine grace and favour and God's miraculous workings':

> what can we less thereupon conclude, than that God would at leastwise by tract of time teach the world, that the thing which he blesseth, defendeth, keepeth so strangely, cannot choose but be of him? Wherefore, if any refuse to believe us disputing for the verity of religion established, let them believe God himself thus miraculously working for it, and wish life even for ever and ever unto that glorious and sacred instrument whereby he worketh.[24]

Richard Bancroft referred to 'those most learned men, and many of them godly Martyrs, who were the chief penners and approvers of the communion book, in *king Edward's* time.'[25] Lancelot Andrewes spoke of 'Those illustrious men, never to be mentioned without the deepest reverence, whose services God employed in the restoration of religion.'[26] Lastly Ken: 'I earnestly exhort you to a uniform zeal for the reformation; that as, blessed be God, you are happily reformed in your faith, and in your worship, you would become wholly reformed in your lives.'[27] In the seventeenth century the great theological controversies were those between Calvinist and Arminian on Predestination, between Erastians and Free Churchmen, between Episcopalians, Presbyterians, and Independents. The way of salvation through Christ and His Cross by faith was disputed by a tiny few.

Some reckon this period as being an extensive modification of the Reformation Settlement in England, and a casting off of ties with her continental brothers and sisters. In fact Anglicans were far kinder to them than the Nonconformist down the road or across the street. J.R.H. Moorman wrote:

> If the dissenters wished for the privileges of the establishment, well, they knew what to do.
>
> The doors of the Church were open but there could be no compromise. Continental protestants were, however, regarded in a very different light. Even the High Churchmen in England were fully conscious of their own essential protestantism, and looked upon members of the reformed Churches of Europe as their fellows. Fear of Rome was so strong that all who had cast off the Roman yoke in the sixteenth century felt themselves drawn together in alliance against a common enemy, however much they might differ in other ways. Moreover in the protestant

world the Church of England was looked up to as 'the chief and most flourishing of all the protestant Churches'. It was therefore customary for members of the continental Churches, whether Lutheran or Calvinist, to communicate at Anglican altars in England and for English Churchmen to worship with Calvinists in France and Holland or with Lutherans in Germany. Even a High Churchman like Dean Granville of Durham had no scruples about communicating with French protestants, and Bishop Ken warmly welcomed the Huguenots to England when Louis XIV drove them out of their native land.[28]

To talk of an Evangelical Succession in this period is really to talk of adherence to Reformation truth and this certainly existed throughout. On the questions of ministry, church polity, fixed liturgy, ceremonies, there was violent disagreement. But the fundamental Trinitarian, Christological, and soteriological doctrines were only attacked by a few. During the century zeal for the gospel was overtaken by zeal between factions in the Civil War. After the Commonwealth, zeal was a less desirable commodity and by the early eighteenth century positively loathed. Within the Church of England at the Restoration it is true the foundations of the English Reformation were faithfully re-laid. It is not evangelicals who have been subsequently embarrassed by the Book of Common Prayer, the Ordinal, the Homilies, and the Articles, to say nothing of the bonus of the Authorized Version. The very century which saw the emphasis change from justification by faith to justification by works, from revelation to reason, from grace to nature, from ardour to entrenchment, saw also the reinstatement of the Protestant heritage. But it must be noted that the numbers of true evangelicals in spirit, active evangelicals with an apostolic enthusiasm, the true heirs of Cranmer, Latimer, Ridley, Bilney, and their ilk, were to be found increasingly outside the Church of England. Meantime however seeds were being sown in this unhappy decline which were to bear glorious fruit in the time of Whitefield and the Wesleys and other participants in the Evangelical Revival.

V. ANGLICAN EVANGELICALISM IN THE NINETEENTH CENTURY

The Rev. D.S. Allister, M.A.
Assistant Curate, St. George's, Hyde

This paper is in three main sections, to enable us to see the subject in broad perspective, and also to focus in detail on particular features without losing sight of their origins in and importance to the overall picture.

First, I shall point out some of the main features of Anglican Evangelicalism in the nineteenth century. This will be done in terms of generalisation and simplification, but that is necessary if we are to appreciate the details which will follow. The second section will look more closely at some of the main characters in the story, personalising and partly explaining the period. Thirdly, we shall see the deeper realities by looking at the doctrinal issues of the century.

The Times
To most historians, if not to mathematicians, the nineteenth century lasted from the French Revolution of 1789 to the outbreak of the First World War in 1914. Although my understanding of centuries is the mathematical one, we must begin with the French Revolution. For the events in France, more than anything else, shaped the emotional and intellectual climate in England at the start of the nineteenth century. On January 31, 1793, France had declared war on Britain, and at the turn of the century Britain was fighting for survival.

Although many Britons had been sympathetic to the Revolution's aims the fact that France seemed to have changed for the worse decreased their sympathy and the war removed it altogether. The prevailing climate in England was one of intensely strong anti-Jacobin feeling.

That was vital for the Church. In the eighteenth century Protestantism·had little influence on the richer classes or the mainly latitudinarian established Church. But, as Trevelyan wrote:

when those classes saw their privileges and possessions threatened by Jacobin doctrines from across the Channel, a sharp revulsion from French 'atheism and deism' prepared a favourable soil for greater 'seriousness' among the gentry. Indifferentism and latitudinarianism in religion now seemed seditious.[1]

So the upper classes, and parts of the Church of England, were to some extent prepared for a return to orthodoxy.

But it was not only atheism and doctrinal woolliness which were seditious: so was any hankering after political or social change. And society certainly needed to be changed. There was an enormous contrast between the wealth of some and the squalor of others; there was a vast increase in crime, and punishment was savage; the ruling classes were frightened of the lower orders; and even the good-hearted among the rich saw the sufferings of the poor as necessary.

The main achievement of Anglican evangelicalism in the early nineteenth century was the improvement of society in these and other respects, and its main method was the mobilization of the upper classes and their wealth in its cause. The scale of evangelical involvement in social change is far too great to estimate, as we shall see when we look at Wilberforce and Shaftesbury. It was the hard work of these men, and the respect in which they were held, which ensured that at least some form of biblical Christianity had a greater influence on the counsels of the nation than at any other time since the Protectorate of Cromwell. Christianity was respected and accepted among the great as well as the middle classes; its influence was felt in the factories as well as the Universities.

But Dr. Vidler is right to point out that: 'It would be truer to say that the age was one of religious seriousness than of faith. No considering man felt able to ignore the question of religious belief, as is easily done today.'[2] The depth of this seriousness can be seen in family life and in business attitudes. In the home: 'Not only a modified Sunday observance, but Bible reading and family prayers were common until near the end of the Century.'[3] And: 'If one asks how nineteenth-century English merchants earned the reputation of being the most honest in the world (a very real factor in the nineteenth-century primacy of English trade), the answer is: because hell and heaven seemed as certain to them as tomorrow's sunrise, and the Last Judgement as real as the week's balance-sheet. This keen sense of moral accountancy had also much to do with the success of self-government in the political sphere.'[4]

Religious seriousness there may have been, increased Church attendance and building there certainly was, but respect for the clergy and particularly the bishops was in short supply. There were several factors to account for this: the strongly Tory character of the Bench of Bishops, which delayed and nearly defeated the Reform Bill of 1832; the largely clerical nature of the Oxford Movement, which frightened many lay people; the vilification of evangelical ministers by several popular novelists of the time, are perhaps the main reasons for the strength of anti-clericalism.

Society, and particularly the better educated members of society, was more ready to take Christianity seriously than to listen to its ministers. This is borne out when we consider the men involved in the growth of evangelicalism in the Church of England. The Rev. Charles Simeon was of course of major importance in the production and placing of evangelical clergy throughout the country, but if you had asked an informed Christian or atheist to name the leader of the evangelicals you would very probably have been directed to Wilberforce in the first third of the century or Shaftesbury in the second third.

That two laymen should have been so influential in the Church was quite remarkable and is not, I think, given sufficient prominence in most histories of the period. In many ways it marked the beginning of a new era, in which we still live today; an era of 'lay theology'. The evangelical leaders had little or no theological training, or understanding of Church history. Such men, when they are devout and sincere Christians, have a great deal to offer the Church and the world: they can correct imbalances and stimulate original thinking; but they should not be the leaders of the Church.

Their leadership weakened the doctrinal character and the Anglican commitment of much of evangelicalism and laid the movement open to and helpless before the forces of liberalism and ritualism. On the other hand, it also greatly increased the social commitment and involvement of the Church, and its influence throughout society.

But it was not only lay leadership which the evangelicals

introduced to the Church. In the few decades before the accession of Queen Victoria these intense and serious men and women developed the evangelistic and the improving tract, the overseas and home missionary society, the Sunday and Day School, and countless Societies for the spiritual, moral, and physical welfare of the poor. To give some idea of the scale of these enterprises we may note that the Religious Tract Society, when it celebrated its fiftieth anniversary in 1849, had already circulated over 500 million copies of 5,000 separate titles, and was issuing tracts from its central depository at the rate of over 20 million a year.[5] Similarly, by the middle of the century, the British and Foreign Bible Society, only founded in 1804, had 460 auxiliaries, 373 branches and nearly 2,500 local associations, and an annual income of well over £100,000.[6]

In order to achieve such growth the evangelicals sought influence with 'the great'. The conversion of souls was their aim, but the conversion of a wealthy, aristocratic, influential, or royal soul was a milestone. We have an example of this sort of attitude from Hannah More, perhaps the greatest writer of tracts and books for all classes. In 1813 she wrote:

I trust Lady —— will be a confirmed and exemplary Christian. Her rank, her vast fortune, her fascinating manners, sweet person, and engaging understanding, will serve to recommend religion to those who will not swallow the pill till it is covered with much leaf gold.[7]

The sort of influence possessed by some evangelicals, though not necessarily of their own making, is not easy to reconcile with consistent Christianity. One example will suffice. In 1814 a second cousin of Wilberforce, the Rev. Charles Richard Sumner of Trinity College, Cambridge, went to the continent in charge of the two sons of the Marquis of Conyngham. In Geneva Sumner married one Mlle Maunoir; some of Sumner's enemies in England even circulated the rumour that this was to protect one of the brothers, Lord Mountcharles, from the same fate. Sumner thus incurred much gratitude from the Conyngham family, who were in a position to advance him as Lady Conyngham was the Prince Regent's mistress. Soon after George came to the throne in 1820 Lord Conyngham introduced Sumner to him, and between 1821 and 1826 he was made historiographer to the King, the King's private chaplain at Windsor, Vicar of St

Helen's, Abingdon, Canon of Worcester, Canon of Canterbury, Chaplain in Ordinary to the King, and Deputy Clerk of the Closet. In 1826 he was made Bishop of Llandaff, while he continued to hold a prebendal stall and the Deanery of St Paul's. In 1827 at the age of thirty-seven he became Bishop of Winchester, where he remained for forty-two years. During those forty-two years he put evangelicals in almost every office and living in his gift. In 1828 he was influential in the elevation of his brother, John Bird Sumner, to Chester, and twenty years later to Canterbury. Dr. Brown is caustic in his comment on this: 'The total absence of Evangelical shame, regret or even embarrassment that one of their clergymen was raised to the bench in such a fashion is perhaps in itself a kind of indication of the strongly practical nature of this reform movement.'[8] Yet the system was one in which all sections of the church were necessarily involved; Sumner himself appears to have been innocent of seeking office through political influence; and any shame should be attributed to the system rather than the man.

But by whatever means they gained their influences, there can be no doubt it was considerable. By the middle of the century, when Shaftesbury's influence was at its greatest, it seemed that the evangelicals might come to dominate totally the Church of England. But it was not to be. Elliott-Binns points to three main reasons: the evangelicals were too impatient of opposition, and thus drove out some more irenical individuals who might have helped them; they were suspected by the Tory party of friendliness with Dissenters, of being politically unreliable and of being too interested in souls; and they had no real depth of character but were too emotional.[9] We shall see some other reasons too: their lack of intellectual and particularly theological calibre, in particular an almost total lack of leadership potential among the clergy; the hardening of attitudes by Lord Shaftesbury after 1855; the evangelicals' inability to see that a national Church must comprehend more positions than the strictest; and the eventual success of the Oxford Movement in persuading many in the Church and country that 'Catholic' theology and practice belonged within Anglicanism.

From about 1860 orthodox Christianity came under attack from within the Church and without, and in the main the evangelicals were not equipped to withstand. The major attacks came from rationalism, hedonism, and ritualism. The free-thinking movements included natural science, historical criticism, and a change in moral feeling. Chadwick puts the power of such an attack succinctly: 'Natural science shattered assumptions about Genesis and about miracles. Criticism questioned whether all history in the Bible was true. Moral feeling found the love of God hard to reconcile with hellfire or scapegoat-atonement.'[10] Evangelicals were disunited and incompetent in their reply: 'Rigorous Biblicists wrote books of Mosaic geology to condemn these heretics. Six days must be six days. The flood must be universal. The best calculators reckoned the ark at 42,413 tons. By contrast the chief evangelical journal, *The Christian Observer* (1834), produced a series of friendly and balanced articles.'[11]

Hedonism was exemplified and encouraged by the Prince of Wales who became notorious for his sexual laxities, betting, gambling, Sunday evening dinner parties, and his invention of the 'weekend'. But evangelicals could not easily condemn such a man when since their inception the various societies against vice had been careful never to speak too loud against the vices of the wealthy, including the Prince's family of earlier generations.

Ritualism was another major obstacle to the evangelicals as the century progressed, partly because the intellectual calibre of the Tractarian leaders had not been matched, even half a century after the tracts began, and partly because of the persistently vituperative nature of the outgunned evangelical response. The undoubted leader in the campaign of hate was the evangelical (and Tory) newspaper, *The Record,* especially after Alexander Haldane, the son of James and nephew of Robert Haldane, both great Scottish evangelists, began to write its anonymous editorials.

Throughout the century evangelicalism continued to produce good pastors and writers of tracts — John Charles Ryle is probably the best example for the closing years — but the respectability of evangelicalism, particularly in the Church of England, was to decline. Its adherents moved in two main directions. Trevelyan tells us that 'The shaking of dogmatic assurance within the pale of the Anglican and Protestant Churches ... helped the propaganda of the Roman Church, whose undeviating claim to full and certain knowledge appealed to persons who could not bear to be left in

doubt.'[12] Others, of course, preferred the growing fashion —
still with us today — for articulating their doubts as if they
were something to be proud of.

The end of the century saw evangelicalism by no means
exhausted, but replaced by both liberalism and ritualism as
the fashionable expression of the Church of England.

The Names
We must now consider some of the people involved in
Anglican evangelicalism in the last century.

Charles Simeon, whose ministry in Cambridge covered the
last twenty years of the eighteenth century and the first
thirty-five of the nineteenth, had, and still has, an enormous
influence on the whole Church. Adored and esteemed,
abhorred and despised, throughout his life and since his
death, Simeon was widely known as 'the Old Apostle'. Above
all he wanted to be known as a biblical Anglican: 'The
Church of England, Protestant and Reformed, was for
Simeon ordained by God to be his worshipping community in
this land'.[13]

Although an unashamed evangelical, and in many respects
the father of modern homiletics, Simeon's devotion to the
Church of England was unwavering, and expressed itself
both positively and negatively. Positively we may note two
incidents to do with bishops of whose theology he
disapproved. One of Simeon's many young proteges, William
Carus Wilson — later to become famous as a writer of
deathbed-scene tracts for children, and, according to Mrs.
Gaskell, as the Bronte girls' 'bugbear for two fateful years'[14]
— was refused ordination by the Bishop of Chester because of
his excessive and blatant Calvinism. Wilson urged Simeon to
object and persuade the Bishop to relent. The Old Apostle
wrote that 'The Bishop has acted a most unjustifiable part'
but added 'I believe he meant to do right';[15] he counselled
Wilson not to object. It should be added, however, that Simeon
was able to resort to Bishop Mansel to get him ordained[16] but
not without lecturing the young man 'on the double folly of
being so rigid and letting it be known to an early
nineteenth-century prelate professionally ill-equipped to cope
with theological niceties'.[17]

A second example of Simeon's belief in the rights of bishops
concerns his own death, for in 1836 a new bishop was

appointed to Ely and Simeon insisted, despite his frailty, on making the then unhealthy journey to pay his respects to his new diocesan. That journey led directly to his deathbed.

But Simeon's attitude to the Church of England was not only one of positive obedience; he also believed that any alternative to the established Church was quite unacceptable: 'There is in Dissent a spirit of disunion'[18] and 'Dissent is an evil'[19] are two of his sentences which express this very clearly. He did not object personally to dissenters, and indeed was most cordial in his relations with Nonconformist evangelicals, but his influence, especially on his own Cambridge men, was considerable. Trevelyan argues that,

Had it not been for Simeon, the evangelical clergy would have continued to drift into Dissent, as the easier method of conducting a peripatetic mission after the manner of Wesley, athwart the bounds of the parish system and in defiance of Church order. If this movement had continued in the new Century the Church of England might perhaps have fallen when the tempest of 'Reform' blew high in the 'thirties. But the Simeonite clergy, though friendly to Dissenters, effectively defended the Church whose mission to souls they did so much to revive.[20]

Although Simeon's obedience to authority was such that he 'refused to have prayers at his religious meetings lest he disobey the conventicle act'[21] he certainly did not use his considerable influence, talents, and resources merely to preserve the *status quo*. He bought up many livings and advowsons and encouraged wealthy evangelicals to use their money in this way to secure an evangelical presence and succession in parishes throughout the country. The Simeon Trust is, of course, still with us.

Doctrinally Simeon was a moderate Calvinist, although he was quick to reject such labels, especially when they might lead to disunion among the evangelicals, as we shall see when we come to look at the Arminian-Calvinist controversy.

Apart from Simeon, and Isaac Milner (also of Cambridge), the leading evangelicals at the beginning of the century were laymen, and the leading evangelical layman was undoubtedly William Wilberforce.

Wilberforce was the only one of those who had supported Pitt in 1784 who eventually received no sinecure, held no office, had no pension and was not raised to the peerage. He was undoubtedly wealthy and married into a fortune, but his name appears on the subscription lists of over seventy evangelical societies, and there are numerous testimonies to generous private gifts from his hands.

Wilberforce's influence, like Simeon's, was enormous, though he is not so much remembered for the many aristocrats and wealthy individuals who were converted through him, or for his overwhelming generosity, as for his tireless work in social causes, particularly the abolition of slavery — for which he conducted, often single-handed, a thirty-year crusade.

But he was neither popular with, nor supported by, all evangelicals. Wilberforce had two over-riding ambitions: to banish the moral and social evils of this country and to spread the Gospel abroad, especially to India. His chosen method, to which he believed God had called him, and for which he was admirably suited, was to mobilize the wealthy. To do this it was necessary, to put it bluntly, to be nice to them. And Wilberforce was charming. Beloved of the Prince Regent, who was to become King George IV, he persuaded him to allow his name to add the ultimate respectability to the London Female Penitentiary — despite the fact that he was a notorious debauchee. If people, their names, or their wealth, might prove 'useful' then Wilberforce, Hannah More, the Clapham Sect, and their allies, would do all in their power to use them. But most of the evangelical clergy at the turn of the century were strict Calvinists whose talk about the wealthy was hardly likely to persuade them to put their resources at the disposal of the Church.

One of those who disapproved of Wilberforce was the Rev. Robert Storry, who told the Eclectic Society in April, 1806: 'We are sometimes tempted to accommodate the representation of evangelical truth to great hearers. But — *I am the voice of one crying in the wilderness*. My business is with the middle and the poor'.[22] Others, such as Joseph Milner, Venn, and Romaine would have agreed. Perhaps the most notable of the old school of preachers to the working classes was Rowland Hill, whose preaching ministry extended from 1766 to 1832. We may admire their consistency and faithfulness to Reformation doctrine and their unwillingness to 'accommodate', but we should also remember that they made little effort to get alongside the wealthy with the offer of salvation.

Wilberforce's successor as lay leader of the evangelicals was Anthony Ashley Cooper, later to become the seventh Earl of Shaftesbury. He was the driving force in Evangelicalism, for good and bad, for fifty years from the death of Wilberforce in 1833.

Shaftesbury may well have been what is now described as a manic depressive. Florence Nightingale, one of his more sympathetic contemporaries, was forced to conclude that Lord Shaftesbury 'would have been in a lunatic asylum if he had not devoted himself to reforming lunatic asylums'.[23] He was certainly a man who experienced acute depression and whose work load was quite extraordinary.

The main spiritual influence on him was undoubtedly that of the Rev. Edward Bickersteth, whom he met in 1835. Bickersteth seems to have been a most attractive personality, without many powers of leadership, but exercising considerable influence among evangelicals. A memorial pamphlet describes 'his irrepressible natural buoyancy', 'his cheerful gaiety in general society', and notes his activities as a peacemaker: 'the waves of vehement argument were often calmed down by the oil of Mr Bickersteth's affection.'[24] Shaftesbury himself described him as 'a jewel, and a jewel of the first water' and his letters as 'a balm in Gilead, grapes of Eshcol',[25] and Chadwick writes of his 'enchanting human godliness and little interest in ecclesiastical politics.'[26]

A most striking feature of Bickersteth's doctrine, and of the utmost importance to Shaftesbury, was his eschatology. He had that belief in Christ's earthly reign before the final judgement which is known as pre-millennialism, although he never wished to fix the exact length of that reign. This was fashionable among evangelicals in the 1830s and Shaftesbury 'made the Second Coming and Christ's subsequent earthly reign the point on which all his hopes centred.'[27] He was driven by a love for souls, regardless of their social standing, and by the knowledge that there was little time left in which to save them.

It is a point worth making that the millennium was central to much evangelical thought and practice. Millennarians could be highly respected and influential figures in the Church and the universities. Bishop Baring, for example, chose 'The Millennium' as the subject for his Bampton

Lectures at Oxford.

Perhaps one way to see the influence of Shaftesbury among the evangelicals is by observing his involvement with the six most important of the scores of Evangelical Societies. He was the founder of the Church Pastoral-Aid Society, the President of the British and Foreign Bible Society, Chairman of the London Society for Promoting Christianity among the Jews, Vice-President of both the Church Missionary Society and the Colonial and Continental Society, and actively involved in the Religious Tract Society. Despite the fact that John Bird Sumner was Archbishop of Canterbury from 1848 it is clear that Shaftesbury was the only real leader of an evangelical party lacking in outstanding or distinguished clergy.

In 1855 Lord Palmerston became Prime Minister, and used Shaftesbury as his main ecclesiastical counsellor. Of the eleven bishops, deans, or professors appointed in Palmerston's first ministry, six were evangelicals. This is well explained by Chadwick: 'Cavalier Palmerston wanted simple godly non-theological bishops. Roundhead Shaftesbury wanted evangelical bishops. Most evangelical clergymen were simple and godly.'[28] All the appointments would have been evangelicals were it not for the fact that there were not enough suitable candidates. The relatively few non-evangelicals appointed by Palmerston included the most distinguished and significant for the whole Church, A.P. Stanley and A.C. Tait (whom Shaftesbury thought was the best of the Broad Churchmen, and who became Archbishop of Canterbury as well as a friend of Charles Haddon Spurgeon).

Georgina Battiscombe describes Shaftesbury's tragedy in her very readable biography:

Episcopal bricks had to be made without straw. Had there been even one Evangelical of the calibre of the Broad Churchman Tait or the High Churchman Wilberforce [Samuel, a son of William] to be appointed Archbishop, or had there been a fair sprinkling of able men to fill lesser sees and to exercise some influence in the Church, the era of the 'Shaftesbury bishops' might have marked the opening of a golden age for Evangelicalism. Nothing of the sort occurred; instead, Evangelicalism continued to decline, as Shaftesbury himself saw all too clearly. 'The Evangelical body, once so powerful, is in fact disappearing,' he wrote on April 16th 1865.[29]

As another authority on the period has put it, 'ten years of Palmerston continued to raise the authority and lower the prestige of the evangelical party.'[30]

A leader must lead in war as well as in peace, so it fell to Shaftesbury's lot to conduct the evangelical campaigns against Tractarianism, and later against what was dubbed 'neology': the new theology, biblical criticism, and the new sciences rolled into one. But in fact the evangelicals took very little part in the early debate with the Tractarians. Even after Newman's Tract XC of 1840, which claimed that the Thirty-nine Articles were 'patient of a Catholic interpretation' the evangelical party was more interested in claiming and rejoicing in its own new-found liberty than in doing battle. The main objectors to Newman were C.P. Golightly (a High Churchman of the old school),[31] A.C. Tait (then a Fellow of Balliol), and Dr. Arnold, who was a Broad Churchman.[32]

The struggle against 'neology' centred on three books, *Essays and Reviews* (1860), a collection inspired by Benjamin Jowett, Master of Balliol, which denied the inspiration of Scripture and the doctrine of eternal punishment, Colenso's *Critical Examination of the Pentateuch* (1862), which was just what it claimed to be, and Seeley's *Ecce Homo* (1865), which described the atonement in terms of Christ's generous self-sacrifice without mentioning supernaturalism or substitution and which Shaftesbury described as 'the most pestilential book ever vomited from the jaws of Hell.'[33] But even against such unorthodoxy the evangelicals were unable to withstand with any real confidence, and Shaftesbury agreed to Pusey's plea to join forces, thus weakening his own position in the battle against the now ritualistic Tractarians.

The blame for the evangelical weakness and decline has been laid at the feet of both Archbishop Sumner and Lord Shaftesbury. But in both cases the claim is too much of a generalisation. Sumner's apparent weakness and Shaftesbury's increasingly harsh attitudes (especially under the influence of Alexander Haldane after the death of Bickersteth)[34] were factors, but so were the overwhelming strength of the new liberalism, the intellectual and emotional appeal of the revived ritualism, and the increasingly fashionable hedonism of the prosperous closing years of the century.

A final name which must be mentioned is that of J.C. Ryle, the first Bishop of Liverpool. Ryle was typical of much of the best evangelicalism of the century. The strength of the evangelicals was their pastoral abilities and emphases, and even after his consecration Ryle remained first and foremost a pastor. He was much more interested in improving clergy stipends than in building a cathedral, and although an uncompromising evangelical he distributed the twenty-four honorary canonries and his patronage to worthy men regardless of churchmanship. His tracts sold in the millions and *Expository Thoughts on the Gospels* must still rank among the best devotional material available, both for scholarship and piety. Like the great majority of Anglican evangelicals of the century Ryle was not fully Calvinistic, but preferred the idea of general redemption to any theory of limited atonement, and also held a premillennarian eschatological position.

The Issues

Our third and final major section involves a brief consideration of some of the most important areas of doctrine to have been raised during the nineteenth century, and the part taken by evangelicals in the debates.

We have already noted the strong millennarian emphasis which seems to have been a feature of evangelical doctrine in the period; there are four more areas of belief we must consider: Calvinism, the nature of the Church, the meaning of the Sacraments, and the nature and place of the Bible.

There were two major debates — or rather long-running disagreements — about the Reformed doctrine of election in the early part of the nineteenth century. The first was confined to those ministers who were, or considered themselves to be, faithful to the Calvinistic understanding. This was a matter of the extent to which 'hard truths' should be disclosed. Some, such as Thomas Scott, John Newton and Thomas Robinson of Leicester took a moderate line: 'They are not all proper subjects to insist on, when we preach to sinners, to prejudiced hearers, or newly awakened persons .... Let it not then be thought *carnal policy* to adapt our discourses to the occasions and wants of the hearers, while nothing inconsistent with truth is spoken, nothing profitable held back.'[35] Those who were more extreme included Joseph

Milner, William Romaine, and Henry Venn, who came close to saying that those whose doctrine was not Reformed could not be treated as Christians. John Newton's reaction to this was very clear: 'Though a man does not accord with my views of election, yet if he gives me good evidence that *he* is *effectually called of God*, he is my brother; though he seems afraid of the doctrine of final perseverance; yet, if grace enables him to persevere, he is my brother still'.[36]

Thus the debate widened, to ask whether the Thirty-nine Articles were Calvinistic, whether non-Calvinistic clergy should be thought of as false shepherds, scribes and pharisees, and whether there was any acceptable *via media* between Calvinism and Arminianism. The end of the eighteenth and beginning of the nineteenth centuries undoubtedly saw an increase in the number of Calvinistic clergy. Thomas Scott wrote in 1811:

Within the writer's remembrance, the Calvinists, especially the evangelical clergy, were so inconsiderable and neglected a company, that, except a declamation now and then in a visitation-sermon, little publick notice was taken of them. But now, it seems, they are become so numerous and successful, that, unless more decided measures be adopted, there is danger lest 'all the world should go after them.' And 'in this I do rejoice, yea, and will rejoice.'[37]

While Wilberforce and Simeon were glad to see more evangelical clergy in the pulpits, they were less happy about the use of such uncompromising language and labels.

Although Newton insisted that there was no *via media* between Calvinism and Arminianism, increasing numbers of evangelical clergy claimed to have found one, largely under the influence of Simeon, who declared, 'I am free from all the trammels of human systems'.[38] The debate became more bitter with the intervention of the strongly Calvinistic Sir Richard Hill and others, whose use of vicious and bitter language may have won the battle but lost the campaign. Newton was heartbroken to see such a debate take place at all: 'How pleased is Satan when he can prevail to set those at variance who are in so many respects united'.[39]

Apart from Simeon, the major influence in favour of compromise was the monthly *The Christian Observer*, founded in 1802 by members of the Clapham Sect. Peter Toon writes that, 'It steered a middle way between Calvinism and

Arminianism .... Its religion was "a gentlemanly Christianity" emphasising the practical aspects of faith'.[40] This continued to be respected and influential, and by the middle of the century there were few Anglicans fully committed to the Reformed Faith.

We move now to consider the debates on the nature of the Church, and find ourselves in a most unfortunate area of evangelical history. For, if the evangelicals had been more clear and consistent on those doctrines which they claimed to believe, the early Oxford Movement would have had much less influence on the Church as a whole.

Part of the trouble was that evangelicals were — as they still are — essentially individualistic, setting little store by corporate Christianity. Bishop Samuel Wilberforce of Oxford, a son of William but himself a High Churchman, put it well: 'Our struggle with such men as Lord Shaftesbury is for our existence as a *Church*.... They believe only in separate spiritual influences on single souls'.[41]

The Tractarians not only stressed the corporate nature of the Church, and God's dealings with the whole body: they were also keen advocates of the doctrine of the apostolic succession of the priesthood. Here the evangelicals made no protest. *The Record* wrote: 'We do not deny the possession of the Apostolical Succession by the Church of England; we only attach an inferior degree of importance to it to that expressed by our correspondents'.[42] And *The Christian Observer* agreed: 'we need only express our full conviction of the Apostolical succession of Holy Orders in the Church of England. There is no historical fact upon which we more confidently rely'.[43] Whatever we may think about the doctrine of apostolic succession, it is clear that the evangelicals of the nineteenth century neither understood, nor fully believed, what they were saying. For the fact is that the evangelicals were led, theologically as well as politically, by laymen; apart from a few solid Churchmen like Simeon they were temperamentally dissenters with little time for bishops. Even Archbishop Sumner, admittedly in a private and confidential letter, stated his opinion that bishops were not necessary to the Christian Church.

This evangelical anti-clericalism can also be seen in the split from the Church Pastoral-Aid Society, which took place in 1837. William Gladstone led a group of High Churchmen out to form the Additional Curates' Society, because of the C.P.-A.S. constitution which spoke of the 'appointment of pious and discreet laymen as helpers to the clergy in duties not ministerial'.[44] This break clearly illustrates Shaftesbury's belief in the priesthood of all believers, which went to the extreme of removing the distinctiveness of the ordained ministry. It is a lesson which should not be forgotten that the ministry of all does not mean the ministry of all in every function of the Church.

Connected with the evangelical confusion and weakness over their doctrine of the Church and the ministry is their attitude to churchmanship and particularly to the sacraments. Here we find somewhat loose theology before the Oxford Movement, which did little or nothing to prevent the rise of Tractarianism, and then a gross over-reaction to ritualism which resulted in the jettisoning of certain aspects of biblical and reformed theology and practice.

Before the Oxford Movement Daniel Wilson, evangelical Vicar of Islington, used words to describe the Holy Communion which might have been more carefully chosen, speaking of 'the altar of our Eucharistic sacrifice', and praying, 'Blessed Lord, I am now about to partake of Thy body as broken, and Thy blood as shed for me.'[45] Another evangelical, on the eve of his priesting, wrote: 'It will be a source of unmixed gratification to me, if I am spared to administer the Holy Sacrament of the Body and Blood of our Blessed Saviour to the many devout and faithful worshippers who are wont thus to approach the Lord'.[46] The evangelicals were not Low Churchmen as we understand it today: it was their own over-reaction to the Tractarians which drove them into the arms of the Low Churchmen.

Evangelical confusion and lack of clarity is also evident when dealing with the sacrament of baptism. This was partly due to the wholesome stress on the need to be born again, and partly because few of them took the Church seriously and most seem to have read neither the Fathers nor the Reformers. Chadwick is helpful here:

> They had learnt to press for conversion, for repentance and faith, and to associate the word regeneration with the heart-renewal of the already baptised man. If they were orthodox Calvinists, they were able to attribute saving grace to sacraments administered to the elect, but to none

others. In 1849 most of the English evangelicals were not orthodox Calvinists. But they preferred to think of the sacrament less as a vehicle of regenerating grace than as a sign or pledge or promise of a future regeneration, itself under conditions of growth in penitence and faith.[47]

They tended to shy away from biblical and Prayer Book connections of baptism with regeneration, instead of trying to understand or explain them.

In my judgement the most serious and far-reaching weakness of evangelical doctrine was on the subject of Scripture. That may sound peculiar, in an age when, as Moorman tells us, 'Few churchmen, if any, doubted the inerrancy of the Bible. The Scriptures were the "Word of God", and could not therefore contain statements which were not true'.[48] The trouble was, not that Churchmen of many persuasions believed that about Scripture, but that they were unable to apply their beliefs satisfactorily to specific problems and questions. They were unprepared and unqualified to deal with the growing scientific disciplines and the innovations in the philosophy of science. So when in 1879 Herbert Spencer's *Data of Ethics* suggested that standards of right and wrong might be another example of the results of evolution the church's response was inadequate. Many believers clung despairingly to Scripture, but were attacked from behind by the theologians, while for those in search of truth the church offered little comfort or confidence. When such ideas have been introduced to the world of thought the church is not at liberty to ignore them and carry on as if nothing had happened — that would be to abandon those who genuinely search for truth in the intellectual world and who eventually mould public opinion. Theology, even the old and orthodox theology, must be presented anew for each age.

And the evangelicals both assumed the inerrancy of Scripture, and also failed to produce any apologetics against those views which became common among thinking people and militated against a high view of the Bible. Previous ages had, on the whole, accepted the authority of Scripture, and the Church now proved itself unable to speak to an age which did not. This was the generation in which a doctrine of Scripture should have emerged in the English Church. But it did not, for it was an age when doctrine was neglected by evangelicals and the climate of the age passed by them unnoticed. Morally the Victorian era was a triumph for evangelicals. Intellectually and ideologically it was not.

Conclusion

There are obviously many lessons and salutary points which could be made from the history of Anglican evangelicalism in the last century, but I will be brief.

The Church did well to take advantage of the intellectual climate created by the French War. The openings were there for the Gospel to be presented to all classes of society, particularly the wealthy, and the opportunities were taken — occasionally perhaps with some compromise, but that was probably due to an inadequate lead being given by the clergy. The laity proved that they could be active and effective as salt and light in the world.

But, because of the superficial evangelistic approach of the pious clergy, the laymen were put in the position of having to be theological leaders. In the Church of England, which ought to be known for its biblical Churchmen, the laity should not have been so ready to do this, and the clergy should not have allowed it.

The evangelical clergy did not manage to prove themselves scholars or theologians, although their pastoral work was, on the whole, commendable. This meant that even a revival of evangelicalism could not make as big an impact as it might. When Shaftesbury was able to appoint bishops, the new patronage 'was no friend to evangelicals in the Church of England. It lifted them up from the pulpit or school where they spoke words of life and buttoned them in a pillory of gaiters'.[49] The Church of England needed to be led theologically; no such lead was given by the evangelicals.

This was a biblicist century, paying lip-service to Scripture but ignoring the doctrinal foundations laid during the great ages and debates of the past, and thus unable to cope with the pressures and heresies of the present.

VI. THE CHALLENGE OF THE TWENTIETH CENTURY

The Rev. D.N. Samuel, M.A.
*General Secretary of the Protestant Reformation Society
and Rector of the Ravendale Group of parishes, Grimsby*

Bishop E.A. Knox, in his book on the Tractarian movement published at the time of its centenary, declared that that movement had

> left behind it a disruption within the Church [of England], making that Church almost a collection of Sects held together by Endowments and by a precarious connexion with the State. Consequently the problem which the Oxford Movement has set the Church of England to solve is that of retaining ecclesiastical unity in spite of doctrinal divergences which often amount to contradictions.

He went on to ask:

> Must not the attempt [to retain unity] end in such a minimizing of the value of doctrine as will react injuriously on the whole of religious life? Would not external unity be dearly bought at the cost of shipwreck of Faith? Can a creedless Church be a teacher of a nation and of the world? This is the question which the twentieth century Church has to answer.[1]

There can be few churchmen, and even fewer bishops, who have so perceptively isolated the problem confronting the Church of England in the twentieth century. If we would understand the phenomenon of modern Anglicanism at all we must from the first recognise that Tractarianism introduced into the life of the Church of England an entirely new element, which divided the church in a way in which it had not been divided since the Reformation. Those who lived through the disruption of the Church of England in the nineteenth century were profoundly conscious of this dimension of the problem created by Tractarianism. Bishop Ryle referred frequently to this, and appealed to the consensus of thought and doctrine that existed in the Church of England before the advent of the Tractarian movement. For three hundred years after the English Reformation the spirit and tenor of the church was in essence Protestant. He buttresses this with a multitude of quotations from leading divines on many subjects, but in particular the Lord's Supper, which is a touchstone of doctrine. Ryle freely acknowledges that the Church of England is a comprehensive church, because it is a national church. He recognises the existence and legitimacy of schools of thought within such a church.

So long as the difference lay between High, Low, and Broad, in the old fashioned sense of these terms, little harm was done, but when the struggle is between popery and Protestantism union is impossible. That is because High, Low, and Broad Church were all comprehended under the generic term 'Protestant', but Tractarianism or Ritualism introduced a quite new element which polarized the conflict in a different way and disrupted the Church of England. It was Ryle's contention that these two elements could not exist side by side within the same ecclesiastical pale. One or other of them was in the wrong place. A house divided against itself cannot stand. The presence of Anglo-catholic teaching in the Church of England threatened its very existence.

Fifty years on from Bishop Knox, and nearly a hundred from Ryle, these words might appear today to be alarmist, and unfulfilled prophecy. Is not the Church of England still here? Has not understanding and acceptance of these parties within the church improved? And if the church is not exactly pursuing its way with clear purpose, it is at least muddling through in a typically English fashion. The contention of this paper is that the views of Knox and Ryle were right; that they were not misguided or exaggerated views, and that they discerned rightly the problem that would face the church in the twentieth century. That problem is still unresolved, and (I do not think it is too big a claim to make) the present and future character of the evangelical party will largely determine the future character and course of the Church of England.

The Growth of Ritualism

There can be little doubt that a crisis point arose in the Church of England towards the end of the nineteenth century. Ritualism had been growing throughout its closing decades, and the church was grievously afflicted and torn by the dissension and strife to which it gave rise. Parishioners were alienated from their churches by the introduction of Romish practices and sacerdotal teaching. It was lay people chiefly who felt the full force of these innovations, and who were, therefore, compelled to seek redress. The parson, while he may deplore such practices, is not himself subjected to them Sunday by Sunday, as are the people in the pew. Laymen took the initiative in forming the Societies and Associations that opposed trends and teaching which they regarded as essentially alien to the Church of England. They opposed the changes that were being introduced in different ways, but one means in particular was litigation. Let us make no mistake, litigation was necessary at the time. There are those, who from the vantage ground of history, consider that it was unnecessary and wrong to use litigation. But that is like saying from the standpoint of contemporary democracy that feudalism was wrong. The judgement is meaningless. It had to be. And litigation in ecclesiastical matters had to be; for, until it had been tested, nobody knew what the law was on these questions under consideration.

The findings of the courts, both civil and ecclesiastical, on these vexed questions of Ritualism were important, for they established just what the law was in these matters. Very often the points that they made were extremely fine and judicious. For example in the Lincoln case, when Bishop King was arraigned for ritual practices, the mixing of water with the wine was declared illegal during the service, but the wine might be diluted in the vestry before the service. Lighted candles only became illegal when something was done with them 'which comes under the definition of a ceremony'. While the judgements tended on the whole to go against the Ritualists, and deprived them of the argument that the practices they were introducing were an integral part of the church's formularies and teaching, nevertheless it is clear that the law was applied with manifest impartiality. If a ceremony or practice came within the terms of the law, even if it were against the tenor of the Prayer Book and Articles, it was not declared illegal. Thus, in the Lincoln Judgement also, the Archbishop declared that Eastward position was legally allowable, because a certain liberty in the application of the term 'North Side' existed.

But the definition of the law in such matters brought no peace to the church for the simple reason that the Ritualists to a large extent proved intractable and contumacious. They were not prepared to remain within the terms of the law however impartially or liberally it might be interpreted. 'The Judgement', declared the *Church Times* in the Lincoln case, 'does not profess to affect directly anyone except the Bishop of Lincoln'. It was 'his Grace's personal opinion and nothing more', and it showed 'considerable progress in the acceptance of Catholic truth.'[2]

By the turn of the century, therefore, matters were getting out of hand. The church was deeply divided. The Anglo-catholic clergy would accept no restraints that were placed upon them either by the civil or ecclesiastical courts. Part of the trouble was that the only penalty in law attaching to such recklessness was imprisonment. This was clearly not the appropriate penalty. As Joynson-Hicks pointed out much later, deprivation would have been far more fitting, or even the refusal to prefer the man concerned.[3] But already the leaven was at work in the Bench of Bishops too, and Ritualists, or Anglo-catholics, were being preferred and ordained by the Bishops themselves, so exacerbating the problem. A crisis point, therefore, was reached at the beginning of the present century, and, other things having failed, the inevitable followed. Questions were raised in Parliament and a Royal Commission was appointed.

The Significance of the Church's Failure to Deal with Ritualism

There were many evangelicals who did not welcome the setting up of a Royal Commission on Ecclesiastical Discipline, because they saw it leading to further delay and episcopal inaction under the excuse that the whole matter was under investigation. Indeed, the setting up of the Commission was itself, in effect, the first admission by the church that it could not, or would not, deal with the problem that had been created by the Tractarian movement. The Bishops had failed, the courts had failed, and now Parliament was to take the matter in hand; but this in itself highlighted the inability of the church to deal with what had grown up in its midst in the nineteenth century. The plea has often been made in recent years that the church must be free from the interference of Parliament to decide its own worship and doctrine. This sounds very well. But what we see in 1904 was a marked reluctance to do this, and, in practice, despite protestations to the contrary, the same equivocation and temporizing ever since. It was a failure of will. There was no *will* to deal effectively at the beginning of the century with the problem created by Tractarianism, which in consequence has been an incubus upon the life of the church from that time.

The findings of the Royal Commission
The Royal Commission on Ecclesiastical Discipline sat and heard the evidence and in due time deliberated. Its findings were in the main very clear. They listed a great number of practices as illegal, most of which have been more and more widely used in the Church of England ever since. In particular they drew attention to certain graver innovations, which they selected for their severest condemnation. These were, briefly:

Celebration of the Holy Communion with the intention that there shall be no communicant except the celebrant.

The interpolation of prayers and ceremonies belonging to the Canon of the Mass.

The use of the words, 'Behold the Lamb of God', accompanied by the exhibition of a consecrated wafer or bread.

Reservation of the Sacrament under conditions which lead to its adoration.

Mass of the Prae-Sanctified.

Benediction with the Sacrament.

Corpus Christi processions with the Sacrament.

The observance of the festivals of the Assumption of the Blessed Virgin Mary, and of the Sacred Heart.

Hymns, prayers, and devotions involving invocation of, or confession to, the Blessed Virgin Mary or the Saints.

Veneration of images or roods.[4]

These they considered should receive no toleration, and Bishops should take, or permit, coercive disciplinary action in the ecclesiastical courts. They were practices which lay on the Romeward side of a line of deep cleavage between the Church of England and the Church of Rome. They were inconsistent with, and subversive of, the teaching of the Church of England, as declared by the Articles and set forth in the Prayer Book. Furthermore, in drawing attention to these graver illegalities they did not minimize the importance of other practices inconsistent with the teaching of the Church of England. With regard to these they stated that 'an accumulation of such practices in a service may, under certain conditions, have an aggregate effect which is more serious, and further removed from the standard of the Prayer Book and type of worship inculcated by the Church of England, than the several practices taken singly would appear to have'. Together they 'unite to change the outward character of the service from that of the traditional service of the Reformed English Church to that of the traditional service of the Church of Rome.'[5]

Now all this made very clear, to those who had eyes to see, the direction in which the Royal Commission required things to move, and the deliberate action that needed to be taken to restore peace to the church, and establish its true identity and character as a Reformed Church. There was no doubt in the mind of the Commission. But no such action was taken. It might have been expected that the Bishops, with the matter so clearly defined and stated for them, would have united as a body to carry out the recommendations of the Commission, and put an end to those practices that were dividing and threatening the peace and even the very existence of the Church. But no such action was forthcoming. Instead the Archbishop of Canterbury took steps to obtain Letters of Business necessary to permit Convocation to embark on the consideration of the revision of the Book of Common Prayer, and in so doing opened a chapter in the life of the church which has not yet been closed.

It is clear that the proposals of the Royal Commission were in substance unacceptable to those who were responsible for discipline in the Church of England. Instead of seeking to fulfil its recommendations, a new way was now sought to deal with the Anglo-catholic movement and its allies, and that was accommodation, or appeasement. The Royal Commission had very clearly shown that certain practices and teachings were incompatible with the Reformed character of the English Church. In other words, the Church of England had in the eyes of the Commissioners a coherent system of doctrine and a recognisable identity, which had been imparted to it by the teachings of the Reformation. Its unity and identity could only be preserved by excluding practices and teachings which were inconsistent with this position. They drew the lines as broadly as possible to include all men of goodwill who were in sympathy with this understanding of the church. But the trouble was that the will was not there amongst the leaders of the church to preserve its true unity by maintaining its Reformed character. Many of the Bishops openly sympathised with the Anglo-catholic movement. Appeasement or accommodation was now to be the policy. Plans were made to bring the Trojan horse within the walls. The programme of Prayer Book revision was embarked upon, and the end of that was not too difficult to foresee.

At this point I would like to refer back to Bishop Knox's diagnosis of the problem created by the Tractarian movement for the church in the twentieth century. He saw that the accommodation of Anglo-catholicism could take place only at the expense of doctrine. The attempt to preserve ecclesiastical unity, when you have doctrinal divergences which amount to contradictions, can only be bought at the cost of minimizing the value of doctrine and making shipwreck of Faith. That is not too strong a term for what was to follow. The determination of the Archbishops and many of the Bishops to keep the Anglo-catholic movement within the Church of England, and regard it as a legitimate expression of English Churchmanship, has resulted in all those things which Bishop Knox foresaw. But let us return to the subject of Prayer Book revision and see the outworking of this disastrous policy in that particular instance.

The Progress of Prayer Book Revision
When you have mutually exclusive systems of thought residing in the same institution the only way you can accommodate both, and preserve a semblance of external unity, is by compromise and ambiguity. From the moment, therefore, that Archbishop Davidson applied for the Letters of Business, the ecclesiastical horse-trading, which was dignified by the name of Prayer Book Revision, began. We are now all too familiar with this process. Each side was expected to make concessions in the interests of unity, but chiefly, by the nature of things, the concessions were to come from the evangelical party. Sometimes evangelicals attached conditions to these concessions, by which it was hoped the drift towards Roman practices might be checked; but while the concessions were accepted the conditions were often later forgotten. At one stage in the Upper House of York, some

evangelical Bishops agreed to the use of vestments, on condition that they were to be white in colour, and that the ceremonies of the Mass were to be forbidden. This was agreed to, and a resolution or rubric expressing this was drafted and carried. But at a session held later on, the resolution was amended so that the concession of the vestments was retained, while the conditions which had been originally framed to safeguard it were removed. So the bargaining went on. Reservation was demanded by the Anglo-catholics and eventually agreed to on the condition that the reserved sacrament should not be used for any other purpose than to communicate the sick. It was not to be kept in the open church, and no access was to be allowed to it. In course of time this condition would be conveniently forgotten too, while the concession would be retained.

In all this patchwork of pragmatic compromise and *ad hoc* bargaining there was by the nature of things no sense of doctrinal principle or purpose. After all, that had been set aside by the refusal of the Bishops to carry out the recommendations of the Royal Commission and restore the true identity and character of the Church of England. The matter now had of necessity to proceed upon the basis of pragmatism rather than principle. Who anyway was going to listen to the theologian discoursing upon principle when people were shouting the odds in the market-place? There was a refusal to recognise that deep doctrinal principles were involved in all this bargaining and accommodation, principles that could not be reconciled by the vote of a committee or the stroke of a pen, because they were, and are, and remain mutually exclusive and contradictory.

The Theological Principles behind Reservation
Let us take for example the question of Reservation. On a Reformed view of the Sacrament there is no need whatever for the reservation of the elements of the communion. We feed on Christ in our hearts by faith when we believe the word of the Gospel and trust in Christ as Saviour. Communion is essentially a spiritual thing. The bread and the wine are symbols of his death for us, and we receive the benefits of his death when we believe that his blood was shed for us and his body was given for us. As it is possible to receive the bread and wine without faith, and so have no part or interest in

Christ, so it is possible to have communion with Christ by faith without receiving the elements of bread and wine, if circumstances so dictate that it is impossible to receive them. Because of this the Reformers devised their rubric for 'The Communion of the Sick'. Where it is not practicable to give communion to the sick person

> the Curate shall instruct him that if he do truly repent him of his sins, and stedfastly believe that Jesus Christ hath suffered death upon the Cross for him, and shed his Blood for his redemption, earnestly remembering the benefits he hath thereby, and giving him hearty thanks therefore; he doth eat and drink the Body and Blood of our Saviour Christ profitably to his soul's health, although he do not receive the Sacrament with his mouth.[6]

Important as the sacrament is, it is not indispensable to communion with Christ. Therefore, the whole rationale for Reservation is removed.

But on the Anglo-catholic view the matter is quite different. When the elements are consecrated by a priest in the so-called apostolic succession they become Christ. The body and blood of Christ are really and truly taken into the mouths of communicants, and as Pusey said, 'After Holy Communion you may pray to Christ as within you'.[7] Well now, here is all the justification you need for Reservation; indeed, it is a necessity. To deprive people of the consecrated elements is to deprive them of Christ. It is vital that the sacrament be reserved so as to facilitate its distribution to all who are sick. But it also entails a great deal more: if Christ is really and truly present in the bread and wine, do I not owe Him reverence and worship? Is not worship of the elements in the chapel where they are kept not merely fitting, but of obligation? And so Reservation inevitably opens the door to all these questions immediately you begin to think in doctrinal terms, in terms of principle, instead of pragmatism or mere ecclesiastical politics.

The Consequences of Doctrinal Compromise
It must be quite clear that these two systems are irreconcilable, and you can only bodge up some sort of compromise between them by playing down the importance and value of doctrine, as Bishop Knox pointed out. But this is a most dangerous course to adopt, for what then is the church

to teach about the sacrament? To vain and ambitious men, of which the Church of England has had its share, the sacrifice of doctrine may seem a matter of little consequence, if by it there seems to be a chance of holding things together and advancing the cause they favour. But the helps they have used to undergird the ship have been the rigging itself, without which the ship will go nowhere, but merely flounder and drift. The effects of the sacrifice of doctrine in the early part of the century are still with us, and have deprived the church of motive power ever since.

By the failure or refusal of the Bishops to deal effectively with the Tractarian movement at the beginning of the century and to excise those elements which were irreconcilable with the true genius and character of the English Church, the church has gradually been drawn into doctrinal compromise and confusion. Indeed, those who might have been expected to know better, and to whom the care of the church had been entrusted, deliberately steered it into those troubled waters in the hope of accommodating a movement which was alien to its true character, and whose exponents had shown themselves to be intractable and contumacious.

The 1928 Prayer Book controversy was the culmination of the first part of this development. The policy of appeasement had run its course. A Book was produced by the Bishops which it was hoped would satisfy all shades of opinion in the church. It included very many concessions to Anglo-catholic views — the alteration of the Consecration Prayer in the Communion Service to include the Prayer of Oblation, Mass vestments, the wafer, the Eastward Position, the mixed chalice, and Reservation. But while it was paraded as a Book that was to bring peace to the church, and unite its disparate elements, it contained something which was an explicit denial of this, and that was the fact that it possessed not one Communion Service for the whole church, but two — the one, the old liturgy expressing the Reformed teaching of the Church of England — the other, containing things which, in the words of the Royal Commission of 1904, united 'to change the outward character of the service from that of the traditional service of the Reformed English Church to that of the traditional service of the Church of Rome.'

If any were in doubt about this they had only to read the

comment of Father Woodlock, a well-known and learned
Jesuit priest:

> Let us now examine the changes made in the Alternative
> Communion Office. These changes are radical and they
> seem to me to make the new office a definite approach to the
> Catholic Mass.... certain prayers have been introduced
> which include elements previously lacking and which seem
> to me definitely to bring the service in line with the Mass....
> Anglo-Catholics who believe in the Catholic doctrine of the
> Mass, should recognize how much they have gained in this
> new Office....[8]

The Vigilance of Parliament

But if Convocation and the Church Assembly were ready to
allow the Church of England's doctrinal position to be
subverted by this new service book, Parliament was not. It is
possible Parliament saw the issues more clearly. Its members
were not subject to episcopal pressure as the clergy and the
lay members of the Church Assembly were. They were free to
make an independent judgement on the basis of the feeling in
the country generally. They were also responsible for the
character of the National Church, and at that time this was
still clearly recognisable. They rejected the Revised Prayer
Book not once, but twice, and gave the Church of England a
second chance to recover its true identity and deal with the
problem and challenge of the twentieth century.

The Church of England had been given a second chance by
the vigilance of Parliament and the faithfulness of a small
remnant within, but the leadership had no will to reaffirm the
Reformed character of the National Church. The attempt to
accommodate Anglo-catholicism had been bought at a
terrible price — the price of doctrinal indifferentism. To
minimize the importance of doctrine in order to gain some
specious ecclesiastical advantage is an act of the utmost folly,
for it brings with it its own nemesis in a church deprived both
of power and a sense of purpose. It has been the folly of the
leaders of the church in the twentieth century to look upon
doctrine as so much junk, so much lumber, to be dragged
about. How much easier the administration of the church
would be, how much simpler the amalgamation of
denominations and the effecting of takeover bids, if we did
not have to worry about this archaic inheritance of doctrine!

And so the approach to doctrine has not been to understand it or appreciate it, but merely to make it less conspicuous, to trim it and shape it so that it will fit together conveniently, and preferably out of sight, in order that the administrators and ecumenical statesmen may have a clean sweep.

The 1922 Doctrinal Commission's Report

We can trace this approach to doctrine throughout this century in the affairs of the Church of England, and it is the result of failure to deal with the Tractarian movement. It is not, it need hardly be said, a serious approach to doctrine at all. It is simply an attempt to get rid of it because it is a problem. We find this in the 1922 Archbishops' Commission's Report on Doctrine.[9] What led to the setting up of the Doctrinal Commission was the growing chaos in the Church of England occasioned by the presence of Anglo-catholicism, whereby you could have in two neighbouring parishes flatly contradictory teaching. Instead of recognising that certain teachings had no place in the Church of England, and were too extreme to be reconciled with its formularies, the approach was to accept without question that both had a place in the English Church, and to trim and pare them down in an effort to fit them together; and, if after the expenditure of much ingenuity and sophistry they still did not fit, to leave them lying side by side in a neutral description of what happens to exist in the Church of England. No adverse judgement, however, may be passed upon any view.

I say that such an approach to doctrine is not serious because it derives not from a concern with doctrine itself, but from expediency, from a desire to patch up some kind of political agreement that will serve to hold men of contradictory theological views together. What would our Reformers have made of all this? What can anyone who has a right apprehension of doctrine make of it? Moreover, it introduced an entirely new concept of comprehensiveness into the Church of England, which is very clearly seen in the first condition demanded of those who were to serve on the Commission: 'They must be thoroughly representative of all those parties in the Church, however extreme in whatever direction, which are willing to seek a basis of agreement.'[10] This, in itself, is a formula for confusion. The comprehensiveness of the Church of England was never meant to be of this nature. It was meant to have an underlying basis of existing agreement, which was found in the general Protestant ethos and character of the Church. That was fundamentally true of the old schools of High, Low, and Broad church, as Ryle and others constantly pointed out. But this new concept was not comprehensiveness, but mere inclusiveness; a sort of Noah's Ark concept of the church, where clean and unclean alike find a place simply because they happen to be there geographically, as it were. Theology then becomes mere phenomenology, or sociology. You simply describe what exists regardless of whether it is right or wrong. If you can fit it all together by some convoluted mental exercise, so much to the good. Otherwise you simply produce a descriptive report devoid of any value judgements.

The results of this kind of thinking still persist, indeed, govern the approach to contemporary doctrinal matters. Its offspring is to be found in the spawning of ecumenical schemes for reunion, and in agreed statements on this and that right down to the present time. We are concerned here, however, with the price that has been paid for this contempt of doctrine, and that is now evident all about us in deepening confusion and uncertainty, in the sense that the church no longer has a Gospel to preach, a message to give to the world. Bishop Knox's words in 1933 in which he said that the attempt to reconcile irreconcilables within the Church of England would lead to a minimizing of the value of doctrine, to the shipwreck of Faith, and to a creedless church were prophecy. For us they are fulfilled prophecy.

In all this it may be said that we have neglected the part that Liberalism has played in bringing about confusion of thought and doctrinal weakness. No one would wish to underestimate the role of liberal theology in this respect. But who can doubt that a church which was fundamentally united on the great points of Reformation teaching would be stronger to resist error than one which had been weakened by the deliberate dissipation of its own doctrinal heritage? It is said by some that no Articles or doctrinal formulae are proof against error. But the fault does not lie so much in the Articles as in ourselves. No weapon has been forged which is capable of defending those who will not defend themselves.

The Past Role of Evangelicals

I come now to something nearer home that is of the utmost importance to evangelicals. By the vigilance of Parliament and the faithfulness of a small remnant the Church of England was given a further chance to recover its character and identity as a reformed Church. But it did not take it.

As we have seen, there was no will on the part of the leadership to affirm the doctrines of the Reformation and exclude the extremes of Anglo-catholicism. Indeed, after the decision of Parliament, many of the Bishops determined to act as if no decision had been taken. They declared beforehand their intention not to proceed against any clergyman who used the services of the Revised Book. The highly unsatisfactory state of things which the new book was supposed to cure, therefore, continued and grew worse. The very things that the Royal Commission at the beginning of the century declared itself against, as compromising the teaching of the Church of England and radically altering the character of its services, were allowed to flourish.

In the midst of this organised chaos, however, the evangelical constituency generally stood firm. Some evangelicals, it is true, under episcopal pressure, and from a desire to see peace in the church, had reluctantly acquiesced in the proposals for the new book, but when it was rejected by Parliament, evangelicals on the whole took their stand upon the teaching of the Articles and the liturgy of the Book of Common Prayer. These, they stated, were the true faith and worship of the Church of England, which was essentially Protestant and Reformed in character. In other words the evangelical constituency did what the whole church should have done a century before when the troubles began. It was no arrogant claim that they made, for it had been endorsed in principle by the Royal Commission of 1904, and even Archbishop Davidson had been compelled to acknowledge the truth of this when he wrote in a memorandum on the Malines Conversations: 'It ought to be made clear on the Anglican side, beyond possibility of doubt, that the great principles upon which the Reformation turned are our principles still, whatever faults or failures there may have been on either side in the controversies of the sixteenth century.'[11] If that note had been sounded oftener and with real conviction, the Church of England might be a very different church today.

The evangelicals, then, were simply affirming the doctrinal integrity of the church, and facing the obvious fact that doctrinal opposites cannot be reconciled. What they did and the position they adopted, they did in the interests of the church as a whole, for the sake of the true confessional position of the Church of England. Of course, they were unpopular, and no one thanked them for doing this, since no one ever does thank you for stating things which are unpalatable yet true. But they were not to be diverted by this and continued during the years between the wars, and in the immediate post-war period, to make this claim, both for themselves and on behalf of the church as a whole, *viz.*, that the teaching of the Articles and the Prayer Book were one, that they represented the true theological position of the church, and that the extremes of Anglo-catholicism, together with the Liberal theology which denied the fundamentals of the Faith, had no part in it.

Evangelicals did not write anything weighty during this period, but any of the pamphlets or booklets you pick for that time, up to 1965, will faithfully reflect this position. It would be impossible here to quote widely from them, but J.I. Packer's small booklet on *The Thirty-nine Articles* published by the Falcon Press in 1961 is representative of the position, and also, alas! one of its final expressions. He drew attention to what we have already remarked upon, *viz.*, the growth of doctrinal confusion going hand in hand with the neglect of the teaching of the Articles of Religion in the Church of England. He attributed this to the attempt to accommodate Anglo-catholicism in particular. He quoted Bishop Henson's words written in 1939, 'The Church of England, at the present time, exhibits a doctrinal incoherence which has no parallel in any other church claiming to be traditionally orthodox.'[12] Packer's answer to this was one that was generally endorsed by evangelicals — a fresh appreciation of the doctrine of the Articles; and a recognition of their truly Biblical character, and the centrality of their teaching to the evangel of the English Church. He concluded: 'The Church of England has no hope whatever of recapturing our country for Christ till the theology of the Articles possesses her mind once more, and the gospel of the Articles is preached once more from her pulpits'.[13]

During this period evangelicals showed that, whatever the

rest of the church might choose to do, they would be guided by principle in theological questions. They held that the body of doctrine of the Church of England formularies was a coherent whole, and the worship of the Prayer Book was consistent with it and expressive of it. This was both intellectually and spiritually satisfying; but, more important, it was a witness which they believed the church as a whole needed to its own true doctrinal position, and it was, as we have seen, one without which the church had no Gospel to preach.

The New Evangelicalism
However, within a few years a marked change was to come over the evangelical constituency. How this came about is still something of a mystery, even to many evangelicals. It was rather like one of those party tricks, in which a man's shirt is removed without taking his jacket off. Outwardly everything still looked the same — evangelicals seemed to be what they had always been; but there was something very important missing — and that was their insistence upon theological principle and doctrinal coherence in their approach to any question.

Let me tell you how, in my opinion, this came about. It comes down to this: evangelical leaders decided in the 1960s to do what the rest of the Church had done fifty years before, and that was to come to terms with the Anglo-catholic movement. The reasons for this were, principally, that they no longer considered there was any future for evangelicalism in holding out. The old position of affirming that evangelicalism was the true churchmanship of the Church of England was no longer regarded as tenable. The lines of defence no longer existed; they had been undermined by the unofficial changes of the liturgy, by the official revision of the Canons in the post-war years, and by the lawlessness of the Church of England generally. At least, that is how the case was stated. Experimental services were about to be introduced, and ecumenism was making the whole ecclesiastical situation fluid. The best hope for evangelicalism, it was argued, was for it to cut loose from its historical moorings in the Articles and the Prayer Book and the constitution of the Church of England generally, and take its chance in the ongoing life of the church, in the changes and reorganisation that were coming about. It might not be exactly, 'In it to win it', but more, 'In it to get what is possible out of it'. To do this evangelicalism had to be free from the commitments and restraints of the old position. Thus in this situation, and pursuing this goal, policy and expediency became paramount over principle and doctrine, even though doctrine may be retained as a formal statement of belief. This explains a characteristic of the Keele and Nottingham statements. First there is an unimpeachable statement of doctrine, but the working out of the policy afterwards appears to bear no integral relation to it. How else can we explain the high tolerance of unreformed teaching in the communion service, for example? I quote from the Nottingham Statement: '... we are concerned lest any revision should give greater weight to the concepts of petition for the departed, eucharistic sacrifice or permanent reservation of the elements'.[14] But no concern is expressed for their removal!

This new policy for evangelicals was variously described as one of co-operation with all traditions within the Church of England, involvement in ecumenism, serious commitment to dialogue, evangelicals coming of age, and full participation in the life of the Church of England. In effect it meant taking the same path as other churchmen had trodden before, of coming to terms with an alien element within the church. But, as E.A. Knox warned, this can only be done by minimizing the value of doctrine and making shipwreck of Faith. If evangelicals choose to embark upon this path the consequences will not be different simply because they are called evangelicals. And, if I am not mistaken, we can already see the consequences of this amongst evangelicals today in growing confusion and uncertainty about where we stand and what our role is to be.

Some Pointers for the Future
To draw this paper to a conclusion: what are the chief lessons we can learn from this brief survey of twentieth-century Anglicanism?

The first is, I believe, the paramount importance of doctrine. This must always be first in our thinking. It must never be sacrificed to some supposed advantage or influence or place. A church deprived of clear teaching is but a useless thing as a church. In time it loses even those things it stood to gain by the sacrifice of doctrine, for its influence and numbers and strength decline too. Doctrine is to the church what the soul is to the individual. And 'what shall it profit a man, if he shall gain the whole world, and lose his own soul? Or what shall a man give in exchange for his soul?' How shall a creedless church be the teacher of a nation or of the world? The failure of our church leaders to discern this truth has led us into the state of decline in which we now find ourselves, and we may be sure that there can be no recovery of our strength until there is a recognition of the importance of doctrine and its revival amongst us, until we have an overriding love of the truth.

The second thing is a proper recognition of what true comprehensiveness is in the National Church. It is not mere inclusiveness. It is not simply the combining together of all sorts of disparate and contradictory elements. True comprehensiveness, such as our Reformers envisaged, is based upon a coherent and recognisable system of doctrine. It may be generous in its interpretation; wide and charitable with regard to things not essential or things indifferent; but it must be one, and consistent with itself. It is a robe woven without seam. It is never a patchwork — a mere toleration, or accommodation, or juxtaposition of contradictory views.

The third thing is the distinct character and identity of the Church of England. We must have nothing to do with the view which suggests that any and every theological position is tenable nowadays in the Church of England, any more than we would acquiesce in the cynical assertion that you can find whatever teaching you like in the Bible. The Church of England has a distinct and essentially Protestant character still, despite what its detractors may say.[15] It is certainly not, as some would like to regard it, an ecumenical experiment, bringing together both Protestants and Anglo-catholics in understanding and harmony. Those who so regard it should keep quiet about it, for far from being a success story it is a dismal failure. A proper examination reveals that external unity has been dearly bought at the cost of shipwreck of Faith and confusion of doctrine. No, the Church of England must still stand upon its historic Protestant confession if it is to stand at all. Its future effectiveness, and even existence, depend upon this.

Commitment to the Church of England, therefore, must mean commitment to this ideal, if it is to be meaningful. I am puzzled by the change of policy of evangelicals being called,

as it was at Keele, a fresh commitment to the Church of
England. They were committed to that before, when they kept
steadily in view the Anglican ideal of comprehensiveness
within certain limits of Protestant doctrine. Now,
presumably, it means no more than commitment to the flux
and change of church politics, and the muddle and
incoherence of what passes for doctrine in the Church of
England today. To my mind the role of evangelicals is vital. It
is to bear witness to the essential truth about Anglicanism. If
they *also* should lose sight of the true identity and character
of the Church of England, what hope shall we then have for
the future? Before everything else we need today the vision of
the Church built upon the foundation of the apostles and
prophets, Christ Jesus himself being the chief corner stone.
We need the vision of a church which is at unity in itself,
where there is doctrinal coherence not doctrinal
contradiction, liberty but not licence, charity but not chaos.

Brethren, 'Ye see the distress that we are in, how Jerusalem
lieth waste, and the gates thereof are burned with fire: come,
and let us build up the wall of Jerusalem, that we be no more a
reproach.'[16]

VII. KEELE, NOTTINGHAM AND THE FUTURE

The Rev. R.T. Beckwith, M.A.
Warden of Latimer House, Oxford

I speak on this subject with great trepidation. The Keele Congress, and especially the Nottingham Congress, are so recent that it is difficult to see their significance in any true perspective. Moreover, anything that must be said in criticism of them may well be hurtful to one's friends, however unintentionally. As to the future, it is a perilous business to try to foresee it. 'The secret things belong unto the Lord our God': all one can do, therefore, is to infer possible consequences from present events and actions, and to make resolves in the light of them.

To some extent I must draw upon my own memory, and you must forgive me if I sometimes sound egotistic. I was present both at Keele in 1967 and at Nottingham in 1977, though on each occasion in a private capacity. I also know something of the background of both, beyond what is public knowledge, through the contacts which my Latimer House work brings me.

When I joined the Latimer House staff in 1963, evangelicals were about to suffer some severe defeats in Church Assembly. Canon Law revision was then in progress, and before it ended both stone communion tables and the eucharistic vestments of the pre-Reformation church were legalised, despite stubborn evangelical resistance; and parliament, though appealed to, did not come to our rescue. The reactions of evangelicals to this reverse varied: a few left the Church of England; others said that one need not be surprised at what had happened — it had been inevitable ever since evangelical bishops agreed to white vestments in the years when the 1928 Prayer Book was under preparation; others again said that, though the change was regrettable, the ornaments and ceremonies of the church must be interpreted by its liturgy and Articles, and these did not allow a sacerdotal and sacrificial interpretation of the Communion service and its accessories. This third was the approach that I personally found most helpful. Other troubles, however, affecting the actual text of the liturgy, were on their way. In 1966 the Series One Burial and Communion services (based on the 1928 Book) were successfully forced through the House of Laity, where there was now a much larger body of evangelicals to oppose such things than formerly; they were successfully forced through, despite the prayers for the dead and the altered position for the prayer of oblation which they allowed.

In this period and this situation, many evangelicals began to wonder whether a deliberate attempt was being made to drive them out of the Church of England. Consequently, a conference entitled *Facing the Future* was organised by Latimer House, designed to reassure people on this point at least. It was explained by Dr. Packer at the conference that we were living in a time when all theological convictions were regarded as relative, not absolute: no one was going to force us out deliberately, when what they wanted us to do was to *contribute our insight* — one among many. Reassuring though this was in the circumstances, it may perhaps have misled some evangelicals into accepting other people's valuation of evangelical theology, and inclined them to be content with a tolerated position within a much more broadly comprehensive church — a mistake which Dr. Packer certainly would not make himself. Nevertheless, this is one of the errors which has become common among evangelicals since: to think of their theology as a permitted option, and not as essentially the true theology of the Church of England. It was especially tempting to think like this in the middle 1960s, when all the formularies which enshrined the theology of the Church of England seemed more likely than not to disappear, in the process of Prayer Book revision, re-examination of the status of the Thirty-nine Articles, and above all reunion with the Methodists, a scheme in which everything distinctively Anglican (and indeed everything theological) seemed liable to perish. As we shall see, there is not the same excuse for thinking in this way today.

Keele

By 1966, preparations for the Keele Congress of the following year were well under way. The background to it has been described as follows, in the introduction to the Congress

Statement:

In 1956, the Rev. Raymond Turvey was appointed Vicar of St. George's Leeds. Before long he sensed a feeling of loneliness and isolation among many clergy, including Evangelicals, and began to arrange small informal meetings of thirty or forty ministers at a time, for discussion, study, and fellowship. Within four years these meetings for ministers had grown into the first Northern Evangelical Conference, held at York, and drawing 250 clergy from all over the northern province. A highly successful layman's conference was held in Leeds in 1964, and the following year came the second Northern Conference, again at York.

However, there was still a sense in which northern Evangelicals felt that too many initiatives of evangelical thought and action tended to stem from London, and in consequence the idea developed of expanding the Northern Conference into a National Congress. This was the background to *Keele '67*, and NEAC, as it became affectionately known, began to take shape.

We will pause here to remark that fellowship was from its inception one of the main aims of the Keele Congress, as it was of the Nottingham Congress afterwards. A cynical man might say that this was the *only* worthwhile aim which the Nottingham Congress achieved (though it *was* a worthwhile aim — *esprit de corps* is certainly helped by an occasional comprehensive assembly of the evangelical constituency). However, Keele, in my view, achieved certain other aims as well. To continue:

In May 1964, the Rev. J.R.W. Stott, Rector of All Souls, Langham Place, together with the Rev. R.P.P. Johnston, Vicar of Islington, and the Rev. A.J.K. Goss, Chairman of the Diocesan Evangelical Fellowships, met with representatives of the Northern Committee. This group proved to be the original nucleus of the organizing committee for the Keele Congress. From the start John Stott was asked to be Chairman, and Raymond Turvey Secretary. Additional members were added to the committee as and when they were needed.

First the committee obtained the support and backing of such bodies as the Church of England Evangelical Council, the Church Pastoral-Aid Society, the Church Society, the

Fellowship of Evangelical Churchmen, and the Federation
of Diocesan Evangelical Unions. From the beginning, these
groups were represented in the planning of this truly
national evangelical congress, which was to be an
opportunity both for Evangelicals to confer together, and
also for them to speak to the whole Church. From the outset
the committee had in mind that 1968 would be the year of
the Lambeth Conference, and waited with some eagerness
for the announcement of the official Lambeth theme. It
proved to be: 'The renewal of the church with particular
consideration of the faith of the church, the ministry of the
church — ordained and lay — and Christian unity'; and this
theme was to find expression in and be reflected through
both the preliminary study material and the final congress
statement.[1]

The Congress book, *Guidelines,* was

a collection of major essays by the Congress speakers, the
result not only of individual study, but of 'speakers
conferences' at which each speaker or writer could share his
particular ideas and problems with the team as a whole.
Guidelines was originally planned as a record of the
addresses, but this plan gave way to the suggestion that the
addresses should appear in print *beforehand,* for study
prior to the Congress, and that the speakers should give a
precis of their argument, answer questions, or amplify
certain sections in a much briefer address to delegates at
the Congress itself. It was hoped that in this way these
essays would not only provide 'the theological backdrop' to
the Congress, but that they would also indeed prove to be
'guidelines' for Evangelicals as together they faced the
future.[2]

This change of plan deserves a little explanation, and after
a lapse of ten years there is no point in being secretive about
it. The Keele speakers were nearly all of them men of some
maturity: John Stott, James Atkinson, Alec Motyer, Philip
Hughes, William Leathem, Norman Anderson, A.T.
Houghton — Michael Green was the only really young man
among them. The book containing their addresses was edited
by Dr. Packer. But when the Congress assembled, the
speakers and their papers took quite second place to the task
of preparing the Keele Statement; and the draft of the
Statement, which was prepared in advance, had been drawn

up at the insistence of certain young activists of unconventional views, who prepared three of the six sections of the draft themselves. Ten years later, it was the same young men, and people of like mind, who largely organized the Nottingham Congress and who both produced much of the draft Statement and were prominent on the platform. Of course, on both occasions the draft was considerably altered by the good sense of the delegates (indeed, at Nottingham there was often more good sense coming from the floor than from the platform), but the man who draws up the draft has an initial advantage. As the proverb says, you cannot make a silk purse out of a sow's ear. The element of stage-management in both congresses must not, then, be underestimated.

Incidentally, the section of the Keele Statement entitled 'The Church and its Message', and that of the Nottingham Statement entitled 'Jesus Christ the Lord', much the most satisfactory parts of the two statements, were drafted by Dr. Packer.

To resume once more:

Meanwhile publicity for the Congress had been attracting much attention, and registrations of the first delegates began to arrive on the Secretary's desk. At the 1967 Islington Clerical Conference the Congress Chairman outlined some of his hopes and plans for the coming congress and voiced his opinion on developing trends in the Church of England in general and amongst Evangelicals in particular:

'The Church of England is changing. Indeed, it is in a state of ferment — although it remains to be seen whether fermentation will result in a mature vintage. On the other hand, Evangelicals in the Church of England are changing too. Not in doctrinal conviction (for the truth of the gospel cannot change), but ... in stature and in posture. It is a tragic thing, however, that Evangelicals have a very poor image in the Church as a whole. We have acquired a reputation for narrow partisanship and obstructionism. We have to acknowledge this, and for the most part we have no one but ourselves to blame. We need to repent and to change. As for partisanship, I for one desire to be rid of all sinful 'party spirit'. *Evangelical* is not a party word, because the gospel as set forth in the New Testament is not, and never can be, a party matter. We who love the adjective *evangelical*, because it declares us to be gospel-men, must take great care, therefore, that what we are seeking to defend and champion is the gospel in its biblical fulness and not some party shibboleth or tradition of doubtful biblical pedigree.'

In answer to a provocative editorial comment in the *Church of England Newspaper*, he assured the conference that Keele would 'not, repeat not, be a string of platitudinous generalities'.[3]

John Stott has more than once since expressed this sentiment even more strongly by saying that 'evangelicals ought to be conservative on the Bible and radical on everything else'. His meaning doubtless is that they should be prepared, *if necessary*, to be radical on everything else, but many seem to have taken his words literally, making it a point of honour to be radical on everything else, whether or not it is necessary, whether or not it is desirable. So it is hardly surprising that some of them cease to be conservative even on the Bible.

I have said that the Keele Congress did in my view achieve some useful results, apart from affording a unique opportunity for fellowship with other evangelicals. It compelled the church authorities to see that *conservative* evangelicals and their beliefs could no longer be ignored. It had previously tended to be assumed that *liberal* evangelicals were the only ones who mattered, and that they could speak for the rest. The second thing the congress did was to compel conservative evangelicals in general (not just a minority of them, as previously) to face up to pressing issues like Prayer Book revision, relations with other denominations, pastoral reorganization and the church's duty to society, which had tended to be neglected in the simple pursuit of evangelistic and pastoral aims, and on which the views of evangelicals could easily be ignored unless they took a more determined part in discussion and action. However one may regret the policies that some evangelicals have since pursued on certain of these matters, it was right that evangelicals were challenged to face up to them, and not to leave the responsibility in non-evangelical hands.

Nottingham

The Nottingham Congress and its background are described in the congress report like this:

The first National Evangelical Anglican Congress was held at Keele University in April 1967. The second began to be planned seven years later under the joint sponsorship of the Church of England Evangelical Council, the Church Society and the Church Pastoral-Aid Society.

The first step taken by the large and representative Congress Planning Committee was to bring into being a number of 'research groups', whose responsibilities were to isolate the main issues pressing upon the Church , to study them and to propose the person who should contribute a chapter on this theme to one of the three pre-Congress books with the general title 'Obeying Christ in a Changing World'.

The three books were entitled *The Lord Christ, The People of God* and *The Changing World*. Published in January 1977, they were sent to all registered Congress participants, who were invited to send written responses to the eighteen contributors. From the large number of responses sent in, each of the authors, with the help of his group, composed an outline of the main topics raised. Thus, on arrival at Nottingham University, each participant received a 'Draft Statement' which formed the basis of the discussion during the Congress itself.

On each of three successive days, one of the books was the theme of the day. After it had been introduced by a dramatic presentation, the Congress divided into six sections gathered round each author. First, the author was questioned by an interviewer, and then the section broke into small groups, discussed the questions raised by his draft and submitted written suggestions for alteration or addition. The authors then revised their drafts with the help of their interviewer, an independent assessor and later the Statement Steering Committee. The revised drafts were duplicated, offered on the last morning to nine subplenaries for further amendment and finally approved.

This elaborate procedure involved a great deal of hard thought. It enables us to claim that *The Nottingham Statement* accurately reflects the reaction of the Congress to the three books. It also explains why some duplication and even partial contradiction occurs between different sections. Yet the spirit of openness and love in which participants listened to one another, learned from one another and sometimes disagreed with one another was a sign of our growing maturity as a movement. Two further points are:

First, the *Statement* is not a comprehensive survey of

everything evangelical Anglicans believe; alert readers will notice some obvious gaps. The reason for our particular selection of topics has already been explained. Much evangelical conviction is taken for granted.

Secondly, the *Statement* is not an authoritative declaration of evangelical belief. For one thing, each section received the endorsement of only one of the nine subplenary sessions. For another, although we aimed at a consensus where possible, we made it plain from the beginning that we had no intention of concealing substantial differences between us where these emerged. One of the main reasons why some sections are longer than others is that they include a diversity of viewpoints.[4]

Certain points stand out here: the somewhat doubtful claim that the committee was representative, the admitted selectiveness of the subject matter, and the fact that none of the draft statement was discussed by the whole Congress. Nottingham was twice as big as Keele in numbers (2,000 against 1,000) and tried to discuss three times as many topics at centres scattered over a campus a mile long in the same few short days. It was inevitably unwieldy, and almost seemed to be big for its own sake. It is very easy at the present time to be complacent about our numbers, like David numbering the people, and to start relying on ourselves rather than on God. Mercifully, there were enough disquieting things at Nottingham to deter us from being complacent. The evangelical essentials were largely taken for granted at Nottingham, when it had become urgent for them to be reaffirmed, and concentration was almost wholly on other matters. In relation to the Keele Statement, consequently, the Nottingham Statement has to rank as a sort of appendix — an appendix of doubtful value at many points. Weaknesses include the definition of the visible church by baptism, to the exclusion of profession of faith;[5] the proposed opening of the presbyterate to women, though with impracticable restrictions;[6] the insistence on organizational unity between churches, not just doctrinal and sacramental unity;[7] the shyness of calling for revision of the proposed Anglican-Roman Catholic Agreed Statements, as distinguished from mere clarification of them;[8] and the somewhat uncritical adoption of secular political thinking.[9]

The Future

Turning to the future, how do things stand? There are, I would suggest, three grounds for reassurance which we did not have in the 1960s, when our survey began:

(i) *The Position of the Thirty-nine Articles.* In the 1960s, the future of the Thirty-nine Articles was very insecure. Even apart from reunion schemes, they seemed likely to be downgraded, especially as a result of the report of the Doctrine Commission *Subscription and Assent to the Thirty-nine Articles.*[10] The final text which the Commission proposed for the Declaration of Assent to be made by clergy at ordinations and institutions (not that printed in their report, but that circulated to the Church Assembly) was so vague that one of the lawyers there said that it emptied the declaration of all meaning. He therefore proposed a different text, which the revision committee took as the basis for its work, and the final outcome (now established in Canon C 15), though somewhat longwinded, is not significantly different in meaning from the old declaration. It is almost incredible that this is what has happened, but it shows what, by God's providence, evangelicals in the General Synod and its committees can achieve, if their convictions are markedly stronger than those of other schools of thought, and they are united in their concern.

(ii) *The Position of the Prayer Book.* Under the Worship and Doctrine Measure, it is settled that revised services (even when bound up into a book) shall not replace the 1662 Prayer Book but simply be permitted alternatives to it. Moreover, it is the 1662 Prayer Book and not they that are to determine the Church of England's doctrine, so the Measure rules; and when there is disagreement between the incumbent and P.C.C. which service to use, the Measure normally gives preference to the Prayer Book service. This could hardly have been anticipated in the 1960s. Of course, the situation is not ideal. Nobody wants to be compelled, for doctrinal reasons, to use old services rather than new: a choice between old services which express the biblical teaching of the Church of England and new services which also, with equal clarity, express it, would be much preferable. But at least the situation has been stabilized. Moreover, it is now becoming clear that the new services are not obtaining so widespread a following as was anticipated, and that in a few years' time Prayer Book revision will probably have to begin again, when wiser policies, one trusts, will be followed. As

things are, the surveys taken in a third of the dioceses show
that Series 3 Holy Communion has not caught up with Series 2,
and that 1662 is still very much in the running: each new
service, instead of being generally accepted, is simply becoming
another minority use.

(iii) *The Question of Reunion*. Here also, a great change has
occurred since the 1960s. Negatively, the Anglican-Methodist
Scheme has been decisively rejected. Positively, the open
communion table has been formally sanctioned in Canon B 15
A, which admits Free Churchmen to receive the sacrament in
the Church of England, removing the really scandalous thing
about disunion. The main motive for merging denominations
having thus been removed, the prospects for such mergers have
become distinctly unpromising. We have, indeed, the Ten
Propositions under discussion at the present time, but if union
with one Free Church proved impracticable, what likelihood is
there of reunion with several at once being achieved?

For the foreseeable future, therefore, the Church of England
seems likely to remain a distinct body, characterised by the
marks which have chiefly distinguished it since the
Reformation. These are six in number:

1. It is a reformed, biblical Church (but suffering, like other
Churches, from lack of discipline).

2. It is a liturgical Church (but allowing occasional prayers,
and non-liturgical worship outside service time, and with a
somewhat headstrong clergy!).

3. It is a national, established Church (but permitting
dissent, and affected by the shift of power from Queen to
Parliament).

4. It is a Church practising infant baptism (but requiring
personal reaffirmation).

5. It is a parochially organised Church (i.e. territorially, but
largely by congregations).

6. It is an episcopal Church (but with considerable checks
on episcopal power).

In all six respects, the Church of England can truly claim
that its constitution is faithful to the principles of the biblical
gospel. It is our task as evangelicals to seek to make this
biblical constitution a living reality, by repentance, not of our
recent openness to current problems, but of our recent failure to
put first things first, and by faithfully teaching the whole
counsel of God in an unbelieving age.

VIII. THE SERMON

The Rev. D.N. Samuel

And the Spirit of God came upon Azariah the son of Oded: ²And he went out to meet Asa, and said unto him,

Hear ye me, Asa, and all Judah and Benjamin; The Lord is with you, while ye be with him; and if ye seek him, he will be found of you; but if ye forsake him, he will forsake you. ³Now for a long season Israel hath been without the true God, and without a teaching priest, and without law. ⁴But when they in their trouble did turn unto the Lord God of Israel, and sought him, he was found of them. ⁵And in those times there was no peace to him that went out, nor to him that came in, but great vexations were upon all the inhabitants of the countries. ⁶And nation was destroyed of nation, and city of city: for God did vex them with all adversity. ⁷Be ye strong therefore, and let not your hands be weak: for your work shall be rewarded.

⁸And when Asa heard these words, and the prophecy of Oded the prophet, he took courage, and put away the abominable idols out of all the land of Judah and Benjamin, and out of the cities which he had taken from mount Ephraim, and renewed the altar of the Lord, that was before the porch of the Lord. ⁹And he gathered all Judah and Benjamin, and the strangers with them out of Ephraim and Manasseh, and out of Simeon: for they fell to him out of Israel in abundance, when they saw that the Lord his God was with him. ¹⁰So they gathered themselves together at Jerusalem in the third month, in the fifteenth year of the reign of Asa. ¹¹And they offered unto the Lord the same time, of the spoil which they had brought, seven hundred oxen and seven thousand sheep. ¹²And they entered into a covenant to seek the Lord God of their fathers with all their heart and with all their soul; ¹³That whosoever would not seek the Lord God of Israel should be put to death, whether small or great, whether man or woman. ¹⁴And they sware unto the Lord with a loud voice, and with shouting, and with trumpets, and with cornets. ¹⁵And all Judah rejoiced at the oath: for they had sworn with all their heart, and sought him with their whole desire; and he was found of them: and the Lord gave them rest round about.

2 Chronicles 15

This passage is about a religious reformation in Israel. There were a *number* of such reformations in Old Testament times. One of the best known was that which took place under the youthful king Josiah, when the book of the law was rediscovered during the repair of the temple, and the king realized how far he and his people had departed from the commandments of God. Our Reformers liked to think of our own English Reformation under the young King Edward VI as parallel to that. The number of such religious movements tells us that reformation is a continual work. It is not fulfilled once and for all. We can never sit back and say, 'The work of reformation is finished'.

We must guard against the notion of infallibility. This is not confined to Papal infallibility. How easily we can slip into thinking that evangelicalism cannot err. That which bears the name evangelical must be sound. We become more concerned about the label than what is in the bottle. Developments in recent years should lead us to be justly critical of that attitude of mind.

Then we also see that this reformation to which our passage refers took place in *troublous times*. Here also there is a message for us. We must not think that God's work only prospers in times of peace, when everything seems to be propitious to the church. I think there is a lot of this present in people's thinking about the church today. The assumption is, that when we have got things right, when pastoral reorganisation and liturgical revision have put the church back on its feet, then the work of God will begin to prosper again. But God can work in troublous times as well as in peaceful; in adverse times as well as propitious. If he wills reformation it can begin now! He chooses to begin with us as we are, not as we shall be when we have improved. There were wars in Israel at this time, disruption of the nation, false religion and gross idolatry, but God sent reformation.

What do we mean by reformation? Reformation is a movement of the Spirit of God and the Word of God restoring the church and true religion. God uses individuals for this work, prophets whom he raises up, as we see here in this passage. But reformation transcends the limitations of any individual. That is where we recognise its supernatural element. It is not wholly attributable to social influences or human agency, though these play their part. The signs of reformation are when men in different places begin to make common cause and think alike, even though there is no physical contact between them, or even communication in writing. Luther, Calvin, and Zwingli always insisted that they had arrived at their views independently of each other. Reformation is something in the air; it is a movement of the Spirit; it is of heaven not of men.

So much then by way of introduction to our subject. I want us now to trace the course of this reformation in Israel and see its relevance for us today.

First, I notice that *it began with a sermon*. The prophet Azariah goes out to meet the King of Judah and his army as he returns from his victory over the invading Ethiopians, and delivers to him and the nation the Word of God. It was this sermon that was instrumental in bringing about reformation amongst the people of God. Somebody has said, 'If ever I am inclined to doubt the efficacy of the spoken word, I recall the speeches of Winston Churchill during the war and the effect they had upon the nation'. If ever we are led to doubt the efficacy of preaching let us consider what sermons have done in the past.

Today sermons are being replaced by dialogue, debates, interviews, drama, and even ballet. Let me give you two reasons why this should not be.

First, God works through the personality of the preacher. Bishop Phillips Brooks said, 'Preaching is truth conveyed through personality'. The preacher is a man who is pleading with people. Like Lot pleading with his sons-in-law to leave the city of Sodom which was threatened with destruction. Paul puts it in this way, 'So we are ambassadors for Christ, God making his appeal through us. We beseech you on behalf of Christ, be reconciled to God.' (2 Corinthians 5: 20)

An actor cannot speak like that; his personality is essentially subordinate because of the role that he is playing. He is impersonating somebody else. But besides this, play-acting lacks seriousness. It is to entertain. The prophet is in earnest. He had rather not speak at all, but he is constrained to do so by the message God has given him.

Secondly, the Word of God is something which is 'given'. It is objectively over against us. It is something revealed by the sovereign power of God, and is not, therefore, arrived at by speculation, discussion, or debate. Descartes, we are told, spent a winter in a Dutch oven, after which he emerged to proclaim that he had found the fundamental truth of all philosophy, 'I think therefore I am'. But you will not discover the truth of the Gospel like that. The Gospel is a truth of revelation and history, not of reason. Men, therefore, will not learn that Christ died for their sins and rose again by sitting in a corner and meditating or debating. Men will not know it, or be able to believe it, unless it is proclaimed. It is, as the New Testament tells us, essentially a *kerygma*, a proclamation such as that which a herald declares. It is the word from outside the human situation, which tells us of what God has done for us and our salvation in Christ. I remember visiting an old lady in hospital. She was very upset because her friends and relatives lived far away and did not know that she had been taken to hospital. She felt very lonely and isolated and said to me, 'Oh for a word from outside'. That seemed to me afterwards to be a kind of parable of man's situation — lost, without hope and without God in the world. It is only the word from outside that can save him. But that word has to be declared.

We must be true to our Protestant tradition in this. The Reformers understood the Christian ministry to be essentially prophetic not sacerdotal, that is, it has to do with the preaching of the Word not with performing priestly actions. Latimer said the Pope had made salvation, the *scala coeli*, a mass matter. Take away the mass and you take away salvation. But the true ladder that brings a man to heaven is this: the top of the ladder is, whosoever calleth upon the name of the Lord shall be saved. The next step below it is, How shall they call upon him in whom they have not believed? The third step is, How shall they believe in him of whom they have never heard? The fourth step, How shall they hear without a preacher? And the bottom step, How shall they preach except they be sent? Now said Latimer, we may go back and apply the school argument, What applies to the first applies to the last. Take away preaching and you take away salvation.

Is it a small matter that preaching is thought little of in the church today? That wrong views of it prevail? A short time ago it was suggested at a chapter meeting that instead of the invariable Communion service there might be a sermon. The suggestion was greeted not so much with hostility as sheer incomprehension.

The reformation in Israel began with a sermon. Without

preaching we may be sure there will be no reformation in the Church.

Secondly, the reformation was *carried on with courage*. In verse eight we read, 'And when Asa [the King] heard these words and the prophecy of Oded the prophet, he took courage, and put away the abominable idols out of all the land of Judah and Benjamin....' There can be no reformation without resolution and courage. Once we have set our hand to the plough we must not look back. Asa saw what was required. He saw the implications of reformation, and broke down the idols and banished the false worship which had prevailed in the land.

Physical courage is demanded for such work. I am reminded of Luther's statement before the Diet of Worms, when his friends were trying to dissuade him from going because they said he would be walking into a trap: 'Though there were as many devils in Worms as there are tiles on the housetops, I will go'.

But I am thinking here of moral courage. You see where the Word of God leads and you are prepared to go, whatever the cost. I believe that our English Reformers had that sort of courage. They were prepared to go through with the implications of reformation: to follow where the logic of Biblical doctrine led. It was that sort of moral courage coupled with the constraint of faith which impelled Luther to utter the words, 'Here I stand, I can do no other; so help me God'. He saw where the Reformation led and was prepared to go through with it to the end.

Reformation men must be men of principle not expediency, ready to follow in the steps of Jesus, who saw where submission to his Father's will led and was obedient unto death, even the death of the cross.

Have we that moral courage today? There can be no reformation without it. We must see where reformation leads and be prepared to follow the Word of God. Half a reformation is no good. We cannot live complacently with those things that are wrong in the church or society. There must be a determination to follow it through.

That brings me to the third thing about the reformation in Israel. It led to *the restoration of true worship*. Asa the king under the impetus of the Word of God not only cast down the idols, but renewed the altar and set up true religion once more in the land.

Reformation is not only negative, but positive. Some would like only to sound the positive note. That is, they say we must preach the gospel, but not worry too much about denouncing error. But that is impossible. It leads in the end to syncretism; to the sort of situation that prevailed in Israel under some of the bad kings, where the worship of Jehovah stood alongside all sorts of heathen cults and practices. There are certain things which are plainly inconsistent with true religion and we tolerate them at our peril.

But there is, nevertheless, this very important positive side of any true reformation, just as Asa not only broke down the images but also built up the altar. We must always be concerned, therefore, with the setting up of true worship in the place of false. This will be marked by an emphasis upon certain principles.

First, true religion is inward not outward. It has to do with the heart, with repentance, faith and obedience, not with outward show and ceremonial. Inwardness was one of the great principles of the Reformation. The Reformers had grasped again the Scriptural truth — first make the tree good, and then its fruit will be good. Good works were the fruit of righteousness within. The Mediaeval Church taught the opposite of this. Following the doctrine of Aristotle, it taught that good works make a good man. But the Reformers went back to Scripture and recovered the truth of inwardness. First a man must be put right with God, justified by faith in Christ, and regenerated within by the Word and Spirit of God, and then good works follow as the fruit of this inward transformation.

Secondly, true religion is God-centred and Christ-centred, not man-centred. It declares salvation is of God. It is God who calls, God who justifies, God who glorifies. It puts the Incarnation, the Cross, the Resurrection at the centre of its teaching. It declares what God has done in Christ as the ground of salvation, rather than what man must do. 'That which exalts God and abases man is the test of a good theology,' said C.H. Spurgeon.

Thirdly, true religion is living religion not dead religion. It speaks of lively faith and trust, and is not satisfied with mere assent. It speaks in personal tones — 'the Son of God who loved *me* and gave himself for *me*' — and emphasises that it is by personal faith we appropriate the promises of God.

Thus any reformation in the church will be distinguished by these marks, and will lead to the building up of true worship and faith in the church, as Asa built up the true altar and destroyed the false gods.

Now we notice fourthly in this passage that, as the reformation continued, so *they began to receive converts from Israel.* Israel and Judah, you will remember, were divided at this time; they were separate kingdoms, and there was enmity between them. But when the people of the northern kingdom began to see what God was doing in Judah and the reformation that was going on there, they began to go over to them in large numbers. In verse 9 we read: 'for they fell to him [King Asa] out of Israel in abundance, when they saw that the Lord his God was with him.'

This surely is the secret of real evangelism. Indeed, we find that it is a principle which is repeatedly illustrated in the Bible. We find it in 1 Corinthians 14: 23-25:

If therefore the whole church be come together into one place, and all speak with tongues, and there come in those that are unlearned, or unbelievers, will they not say that ye are mad? But if all prophesy, and there come in one that believeth not, or one unlearned, he is convinced of all, he is judged of all: And thus are the secrets of his heart made manifest; and so falling down on his face he will worship God, and report that God is in you of a truth.

If in your worship, says St. Paul, you all speak in tongues, the outsider will simply think you mad. But if the Word of God is preached, he will be convinced and convicted. He will recognise that God is truly amongst you, and will come over to you. We find the same thing again in the book of Zechariah (8: 23). The prophet is speaking of the restoration of the people of God in the last times. God will work a great revival amongst his people the Jews with the result that, 'In those days it shall come to pass, that ten men out of all languages of the nations shall take hold of the skirt of him that is a Jew, saying, We will go with you: for we have heard that God is with you'.

This is a general principle we do well to notice. Let us seek a genuine work of God in the church, and the outreach will take care of itself. So often today the church is concerned merely with the mechanics of getting people in. But into what?

I often see a placard which is placed outside a church and changes every week. One week it has, 'Songs of Praise, choose

your favourite hymns'. The next week, 'Special Flower Service
— Say it with flowers'. The next week, 'Riding on a Donkey —
bring your pets to the service'. The last time I passed there was
a notice which said, 'Concert by the Women's Choral Society,
followed by shortened Evensong'. What is the good of
inveigling people into church on these terms? Have we achieved
anything at all when we have got them in? Should we not
rather say like Moses, 'If thy presence go not with me, carry us
not up hence'? We do not want to enter the promised land if God
is not with us. We do not want 'success' if God is not in it, and, if
God is in it, it must be a success. The fundamentally important
thing is to know that God is with us, that he is at work in the
church. When the outsider sees that of a truth God is amongst
us, he will be convicted and convinced.

Lastly, we see *the culmination of this reformation in Israel*.
'They had sworn with all their heart, and sought him [the
Lord] with their whole desire; and he was found of them'. Is not
that the distinguishing mark of true reformation? That people
seek God with their whole heart? In every great awakening
which we read of, either in Biblical times or church history, the
great question which begins to agitate men's minds is, How can
I find a gracious God? I could cite many examples of this, but
one comes to mind from my own reading. John Cennick was a
contemporary of the Wesleys. In the 1740s, at the beginning of
the Evangelical Awakening, he began to seek God. He relates
how he could not rest until he had found the way of salvation.
He had heard that there was a Fellow of one of the Oxford
colleges, who was a friend of Whitefield. He felt that man would
be able to help him. So he set out to walk from London to
Oxford. When he got to Oxford he had to go round all the
colleges and enquire after this man, for he was not sure of his
name. He sought the Lord with all his heart and with his whole
desire. This was very characteristic of that whole period.

The essence of religion is in seeking and finding God, or
rather, as the Bible says, being found of him. When God creates
soul-thirst, and graciously discloses himself to men, and we
know him as Father in Jesus Christ, that is the fulfilment and
fruition of Reformation in the church.

May God in his mercy grant us such reformation in these
days, times of refreshing from the presence of the Lord.

REFERENCES

I Introduction

1   Psalm 77: 10 (Prayer Book)

II The Theology of the English Reformers

1   John 17: 3
2   W.H. Griffith Thomas, *Principles of Theology* (1956 edition), 101-2
3   Archbishops' Commission on Christian Doctrine, *Subscription and Assent to the 39 Articles* (1968), 16
4   H.Christmas (Ed.), *Works of Nicholas Ridley* (Parker Society; 1843), 16
5   J.Ayre (Ed.), *Works of John Jewel* (Parker Society; 1845-50), I, 80
6   Cf. English Church Tracts, No. 10, *What the Church of England stands for*
7   J. Barr, *Fundamentalism* (1977), 343-4
8   Cf. *Authority in the Church: A criticism of the Anglican-Roman Catholic Agreed Statement* (Protestant Reformation Society; 1977)
9   *Authority in the Church* (1977), paragraph 2
10 J.E. Cox (Ed.), *Thomas Cranmer on the Lord's Supper* (1844; Parker Society), 23-4
11 C.O. Buchanan, E.L. Mascall, J.I. Packer, G.D. Leonard, *Growing into Union* (1970), 38
12 G.L.Bray, 'NEAC Critique', in *Third Way*, Vol. 1, No. 10, May 19, 1977, p.21
13 J.I. Packer, *'Fundamentalism' and the Word of God* (1958), 112-3
14 The Doctrine Commission of the Church of England, *Christian Believing* (1976), 9
15 Bray, *op.cit.,* 21
16 W. Whitaker, *A Disputation on Holy Scripture* (1849; Parker Society), 359
17 Jewel, II, 683
18 'A Fruitful Exhortation to the Reading and Knowledge of Holy Scripture', ii
19 Whitaker, 361-2; cf. 363
20 Whitaker, 376
21 Whitaker, 392
22 Jewel, I, 331
23 Cf. Whitaker, 374 and 400; and Jewel, II, 684
24 'A Fruitful Exhortation to the Reading and Knowledge of Holy Scripture', ii
25 Whitaker, 364
26 G.G.E.A. Dix, *The Shape of the Liturgy* (1945), 672
27 J.I. Packer, 'Gain and Loss', in R.T. Beckwith (Ed.), *'Towards a Modern Prayer Book* (1966), 76
28 'An Homily of the worthy receiving and reverent esteeming of the Sacrament of the Body and Blood of Christ', i
29 Packer, 'Gain and Loss', 88-89
30 Article XXVIII
31 A. Townsend (Ed.), *The Writings of John Bradford*, I (1848; Parker Society), 108
32 Article XXVIII; Article XXIX
33 Jewel, III, 558-9
34 J.T. Tomlinson, *The Great Parliamentary Debate in 1548, on the Lord's Supper* (Second edition; n.d.), 27 and 39
35 Jewel, II, 1101
36 Ridley, 9; cf. J. Ayre (Ed.), *The Sermons of Edwin Sandys* (1842; Parker Society), 90

37 P. Crowe (Ed.), *Keele '67* (1967), 35; cf. J.R.W. Stott (Ed.), *The Nottingham Statement* (1977), 24
38 T.Russell (Ed.), *The Works of the English Reformers: William Tyndale, and John Frith*, III (1831), 446-7
39 C.O. Buchanan (Ed.), *Evangelical Essays on Church and Sacraments* (1972), 60
40 Jewel, I, 230; cf. 6-7. It is clear that the Reformers used the word *infant* not in its narrow sense of a babe in arms, but in the wider sense of a child.
41 T. Harding (Ed.), *The Decades of Henry Bullinger* (1849-52; Parker Society), IV, 426
42 Bullinger, III, 398
43 W. Nicholson (Ed.), *Remains of Edmund Grindal* (1843; Parker Society), 162-3. Other injunctions which imply that none younger than a 'young man or woman' were to partake are: J. E. Cox (Ed.), *Miscellaneous Writings and Letters of Thomas Cranmer* (1846; Parker Society), 82; G.E Corrie (Ed.), *Sermons and Remains of Hugh Latimer* (1844-5 Parker Society), II, 243; C. Nevinson (Ed.), *Later Writings of Bishop Hooper* (1852; Parker Society), 132
44 *The Churchman*, LXXXV (1971), 30
45 *Growing into Union*, 55
46 Buchanan, *op.cit.*, 52
47 Article XIX
48 J. Ayre (Ed.), *The Catechism of Thomas Becon* (1844; Parker Society), 320
49 Latimer, I, 306
50 H. Walter (Ed.), *Doctrinal Treatises by William Tyndale* (1848; Parker Society), 284
51 Latimer, I, 202, and 504
52 Jewel, II, 953-4
53 Latimer, I, 199
54 *Ibid*, I, 292
55 *Ibid*, I, 507
56 Sandys, 350
57 Latimer, I, 70
58 *Ibid*, I, 202
59 *Ibid*, I, 200
60 Sandys, 271
61 Latimer, I, 528
62 Acts 6: 2 & 4
63 Latimer I, 202, and 306
64 Philip Edgcumbe Hughes, *Theology of the English Reformers* (1965), 156
65 Hughes, *op.cit.*, 158
66 Latimer, I, 487
67 *Loc. cit.*
68 John Foxe, *Acts and Monuments* (1843-49 edition), VII, 550
69 Ephesians 1: 6

III Doctrinal Continuity in the Century after the Reformation

1 J.C. Ryle, *The Christian Leaders of the Last Century* (1869), 15
2 Joseph Butler, *The Analogy of Religion, Natural and Revealed* (1736), Advertisement [Everyman edition, p. 1]
3 R.S. Hardy, *William Grimshaw* (1860), 174
4 Ryle, *op.cit.*, 379-80
5 *The Works of Augustus Toplady* (1837 edition), 3
6 Ryle, *op.cit.*, 367
7 *Works*, 46
8 *Works*, 124
9 *Works*, 614
10 *Works*, 129

11 *Works*, 128-9. Cf. J. Ketley (Ed.), *The Two Liturgies ... with other documents ... of King Edward VI* (1844; Parker Society), 511-12 (559-60), 512 (560), 512-13 (560-1), 503 (552)
12 *Works*, 126
13 *Works*, 133
14 *Works*, 140. Cf. G.E. Corrie (Ed.), *Sermons and Remains of Hugh Latimer* (1844-5; Parker Society), I, 330
15 *Works*, 141. Cf. Latimer, II, 137
16 *Works*, 196
17 *Works*, 196
18 *Works*, 198-9
19 *Works*, 200; Grindal to Bullinger, August 27, 1566. Cf. H. Robinson (Ed.), *The Zurich Letters* (1842; Parker Society), 169
20 *Works*, 214
21 *Works*, 221
22 *Works*, 245
23 *Works*, 258
24 *Works*, 258
25 *Works*, 264
26 *Works*, 275

IV From Laud to Waterland

1   G.R. Balleine, *A History of the Evangelical Party in the Church of England* (1951 edition), 40 n.1
2   Balleine, *op.cit.*, 1
3   V.H.H. Green, *Religion at Oxford and Cambridge* (1964), 147 (My italics)
4   J.C. Ryle, *Knots Untied* (1874), Chapter 1
5   J.R.W. Stott, *What is an evangelical?* (1977), 6 and 10
6   Owen Chadwick, *The Reformation* (1964), 424
7   J.R. Green, *A Short History of the English People* (1916 edition), 460-462
8   J. Pearson, *An Exposition of the Creed,* The Epistle Dedicatory [1845 edition, p. 2]
9   C. Hill, *Change and Continuity in Seventeenth-Century England* (1974), 17
10 Hill, *op.cit.*, 21
11 Hill, *op.cit.*, 43
12 J.M. Brentnall, *William Bagshawe* (1970), 19
13 William Laud, *Works*, V (1853), 299
14 H.D.M. Spence, *The Church of England* (1898), IV, 65
15 B.L. Manning, *The Making of Modern English Religion* (1929), 101
16 J.R.H. Moorman, *A History of the Church in England* (1973), 255
17 G. Burnet, *An Exposition of the XXXIX Aritcles* (1831 edition), 167
18 *Ibid.,* 159 (My italics)
19 W. Beveridge, *The Theological Works,* VII — On the Thirty-nine Articles (1845), 292, 293
20 Burnet, *op.cit.*, 239
21 Beveridge, *op. cit.*, 353
22 D. Waterland, *A Review of the Doctrine of the Eucharist* (1861 edition), page v
23 Waterland, *op. cit.*, 174-5 [*Works*, VII (1823), 195-6] Cf. J.E. Cox (Ed.), *Thomas Cranmer on the Lord's Supper* (1844; Parker Society), 328.
24 R. Hooker, *Of the Laws of Ecclesiastical Polity*, IV, xiv, 7 [*Works* (1888), I, 488]
25 R. Bancroft, *A Survay of the pretended Holy Discipline* (1593), 357 (*spelling modernised*)
26 '*Illustres* illi *viri,* nec unquam sine summa honoris praefatione nominandi, quorum Deus, in *Religione* restauranda, opera usus est': L. Andrewes, *Opuscula quaedam posthuma* (1852), 11.
27 T. Ken, 'A Sermon preached upon Passion Sunday' [April 1st., 1688] Cf. J.T. Round, *The Prose Works of Thomas Ken* (1838), 205.
28 Moorman, *op.cit.*, 282

V Anglican Evangelicalism in the Nineteenth Century

1   G.M. Trevelyan, *English Social History* (1944), 493
2   A.R. Vidler, *The Church in an Age of Revolution* (1971), 113
3   Trevelyan, *op.cit.*, 565
4   R.C.K. Ensor, *England 1870-1914* (1936), 138
5   I.C. Bradley, *The Call to Seriousness* (1976), 42
6   *Ibid.*, 136
7   W. Roberts, *Memoirs of the Life and Correspondence of Mrs. Hannah More* (1834), III, 372
8   F.K. Brown, *Fathers of the Victorians* (1961), 62
9   L.E. Elliott-Binns, *Religion in the Victorian Era* (1946), 50
10   Owen Chadwick, *The Victorian Church,* I (1966), 551
11   *Ibid.*, 561-2
12   Trevelyan, *op.cit.*, 566
13   A. Pollard and M.M. Hennell (Ed.), *Charles Simeon* (1959), 162
14   Hugh Evan Hopkins, *Charles Simeon of Cambridge* (1977), 98
15   W. Carus, *Memoirs of the Life of the Rev. Charles Simeon* (1847), 417-18
16   This is the story as told in Pollard & Hennell and in Brown; Hopkins offers a different version in which the Bishop of Ely is the one who refused to ordain Wilson until Simeon persuaded the young man to explain that his views were not as rigid as he thought them to be. But the point is the same.
17   F.K. Brown, *op.cit.*, 463
18   A.W. Brown, *Recollections of the Conversation Parties of the Rev. Charles Simeon* (1863), 222
19   *Ibid.*, 223
20   Trevelyan, *op.cit.*, 510
21   Chadwick, *op.cit.*, 442 n.2
22   J.H. Pratt, *Eclectic Notes* (1865; second edition), 386
23   C.B. Woodham-Smith, *Florence Nightingale* (1950), 589
24   Georgina Battiscombe, *Shaftesbury* (1974), 100
25   *Loc.cit.*
26   Chadwick, *op.cit.*, 455
27   Battiscombe, *op.cit.*, 101
28   Chadwick, *op.cit.*, 471
29   Battiscombe, *op.cit.*, 264
30   Chadwick, *op. cit.*, 469
31   It is important to realise that High, Middle, and Low churchmanship have changed their meanings considerably. Whereas today High is often synonymous with Anglo-catholic and Low with evangelical, in the early nineteenth century all Anglicans were Protestant; churchmanship was more a matter of the importance clergy attached to the Church as an institution, and was of less significance than it is today.
32   G.R. Balleine, *A History of the Evangelical Party in the Church of England* (1951 edition), 172-3
33   Battiscombe, *op.cit.*, 269
34   Chadwick, *op.cit.*, 455
35   J. Scott, *The Life of the Rev. Thomas Scott* (1822), 648
36   *The Works of the Rev. John Newton* (1824; third edition), VI, 199
37   T. Scott, *Remarks on the Refutation of Calvinism by George Tomline* (1811), I, iii-iv
38   Carus, *op.cit.*, 563
39   Quoted at: F.K. Brown, *op.cit.*, 172
40   Peter Toon, 'Papers of Old', in *Anglican,* December, 1976
41   Battiscombe, *op.cit.*, 265
42   *The Record,* December 12, 1833, p. 4, col. 3
43   *The Christian Observer,* XXXIV (1834), 64

44   Battiscombe, *op.cit.*, 104
45   J. Bateman, *The Life of the Right Rev. Daniel Wilson, D.D.* (1860), I, 157 and 284
46   Henry Hutton. Quoted at: G.W.E. Russell, *A Short History of the Evangelical Movement* (1915), 19-20
47   Chadwick, *op.cit.*, 255
48   J.R.H. Moorman, *A History of the Church in England* (1973), 273
49   Chadwick, *op.cit.*, 476

VI The Challenge of the Twentieth Century

1   E.A. Knox, *The Tractarian Movement* (1933), 383
2   *The Church Times*, November 28, 1890, p. 1154 col. 1, and p. 1153 col. 2
3   Sir William Joynson-Hicks, *The Prayer-Book Crisis* (1928), 59-60
4   *Report of the Royal Commission on Ecclesiastical Discipline* (1906), 32-44
5   *Ibid.*, 53
6   Rubric at the end of 'The Communion of the Sick', *The Book of Common Prayer*
7   J.O. Johnston and W.C.E. Newbolt, *Spiritual Letters of Edward Bouverie Pusey*, (1901), 286
8   Quoted at: Joynson-Hicks, *op.cit.*, 144-5
9   *Doctrine in the Church of England — The Report of the Commision on Christian Doctrine appointed by the Archbishops of Canterbury and York in 1922* (1938)
10   From a Memorial presented to the Archbishop of Canterbury in 1922, suggesting the appointment of a Commission on Christian Doctrine. Printed at: G.K.A. Bell, *Randall Davidson* (1935), 1146
11   Bell, *op.cit.*, 1279
12   H.H. Henson, *The Church of England* (1939), 108
13   J.I. Packer, *The Thirty-nine Articles* (1961), 46
14   J.R.W. Stott (Ed.), *The Nottingham Statement* (1977), F3 (e)
15   Cf. English Church Tracts, No. 10, *What the Church of England stands for*
16   Nehemiah 2: 17

VII Keele, Nottingham, and the Future

1   P. Crowe (Ed.), *Keele '67* (1967), 7
2   *Ibid.*, 8
3   *Loc.cit.*
4   J.R.W. Stott (Ed.), *The Nottingham Statement* (1977), 3-4
5   *Ibid.*, 19, 25; but contrast 28
6   *Ibid.*, 33, 35
7   *Ibid.*, 40
8   *Ibid.*, 44f.
9   *Ibid.*, 46f., 51
10   Archbishops' Commission on Christian Doctrine, *Subscription and Assent to the 39 Articles* (1968)

VIII The Sermon

1   Preached in the Chapel of the Old Palace, Lincoln, on September 15, 1977